The Essence of Humanity

by

JAMES GATES

authorHOUSE®

AuthorHouse™
1663 Liberty Drive, Suite 200
Bloomington, IN 47403
www.authorhouse.com
Phone: 1-800-839-8640

Published by AuthorHouse 2/12/2009

ISBN: 978-1-4389-2252-2 (sc)
ISBN: 978-1-4772-4054-0 (e)

This book is printed on acid-free paper.

The Essence of Humanity

I GREW UP IN A hostile society in a complex time. It was a social environment governed by insanity, bigotry, fear, and inhumanity. But beyond the madness, a sense of hopelessness induced a measure of tolerance that created a guarded feeling of happiness and well being, yet tainted by fear.

At an early age I studied the Greek philosophy of Aristotle, Plato, and Socrates. I also studied Darwin's theories, and others. Purely from a profound inquiry point of view, I found the principles and theories to say the least, fascinating, yet mere speculation.

I am a Christian not an evolutionist. I believe that the only rational explanation for everything in existence was formed by Divine Arrangement which I believe to be God. I also believe that when we are disconnected from the creator, the source of all things, we are nothing more than simple animals. This is the only rational explanation for the irrational behavior of the social majority of that era, and human behavior in general.

However, in my observation and examination of human behavior and the characteristics that govern both human and animal social existence, I discovered that some of Darwin's conclusions when applied to human behavior offer a reasonable degree of legitimacy. For example, the survival of the fittest and natural selection were conclusion based on the relationship and social behavior of the animals that he observed. But his hypotheses also mirrored the social behavior of the animal called man, and the way we behave and respond to all environmental stimuli.

As I observed and experienced the blatant inhumanities associated with bigotry and other flaws, I realized that I was in a unique position to analyze the relationship between human behavior, and the natural instincts that govern it.

Throughout this book, it is possible that I may use and modify a few of Darwin's conclusions to support my own. However, I will not allow these adjustments to exceed the boundaries of my own observation, faith and reasoning.

Godliness and wickedness are spiritual forces that govern human moral and social behavior. To define and explain how our flawed, natural instincts are in primary charge of our souls, I searched for a means to examine the two forces. Because these opposing forces are control by either God or Satan, I considered becoming a preacher. But as a black preacher, I felt that I could only reach the souls of blacks.

Even though I recognized at an early age that ministering the gospel was something that I was destined to do, it did not appeal to me at that time. My reluctance was primarily supported by my desire to share my ideas and beliefs with everyone in a non-ministering setting.

Because of the diversity of human social structures, and the variations in religious beliefs, I felt that it would be impossible to minister to everyone about Christianity. So, I decided to create with a poetical assault what I considered as the fundamental functioning of humanity. This method that I chose would be radical and yet rational. All human beings are capable of reasoning, whether we demonstrate the capacity for it or not.

As I assembled words on the pages, I was amazed at how effortlessly they flowed from the depths of my still troubled soul. There were no constraints to handicap my beliefs and conclusions. I had reached a level of consciousness that allowed me to examine, and explore the functioning of the entity that we call the soul.

The words on these pages will not completely reveal the effect that creating them had on me. But from the shadows of mere existence in which I lived, a new image emerged; generating an alien form of rebirth.

As I stumbled through the dawning of my new understanding, I felt no vanity, but a magnificent light shined. It illuminated the path that I had chosen. I can only hope that if any individual read these words, their hearts will be enlightened too.

The Challenge

THE CONSTANT ASSAULT BY MOSTLY external aggression to undermine America's moral consciousness and stability is a testament to its greatness. It also has an enormous racial diversity that exposes the enormous differences in the masses that often generate a great divide. And although the misunderstandings and disagreements have often concluded with irrational consequences, they are the mechanisms that sustain our nation's greatness.

Despite our nation's leadership in the world, in terms of its ambition to force feed democracy to every global community, it still has an infinite number of problems here at home. With our diverse cultures, and radical differences of opinions, it is a constant struggle to compensate for the problems that the diversity sometime creates. However, diversity is an inherited function of the principle of free will.

As we struggle with our social problems, we must also understand that it is not totally our nation's diversity, but the governing by the politicians who oversee our affairs that are plunging our nation into a chaotic state. Our electoral process is the best that modern civilization has to offer. But our greatest challenge appears to lie in our inability to select competent political representation. Course we only have a small group from which to choose. Out of this small group, an overwhelming number of these people are often only interested in using their political positions for their own selfish gains. But because our society tolerates this behavior, the individuals parade around as if they were heirs to a royal throne.

When the checks and balances of our governing bodies are functioning with any degree of parity, our political system is by far the best on earth.

But regardless of our nation's political state of affairs, to continue to totally trust our future to politicians is ridiculous. They are human, and therefore subject to the same flaws as everyone else. In addition, despite their political promises, the majority of them do not have any interest in healing our nation's wounds. It is much too easy for them to apply a Band-Aid, and still maintain their illusions of great public officials.

The individuals that we select to represent us are supposed to be submissive to the wishes of their constituents, because they are only extensions of the people who vote for them. Therefore, as voters, we must not allow them to determine the path that our nation should travel without consulting us.

The conscious of America is its citizens. When there are issues that are vital to our nation's well being, we must unite as a single mechanism, and function as a unit. We must develop the same drive and purpose that motivated our nation's ancestors, as they struggled to construct and protect the foundation of democracy.

The wombs of the world's communities conceived and established the foundation of America with its many cultures, colors and beliefs. In order to retain the freedoms that we have, the diversity in our nation must become an enormous indivisible rainbow of strength.

We still consider the evils of communism, and any society that supports its doctrine as the greatest enemies to democracy. The citizens living under these regimes are taught just the opposite. The seemly infinite barrier that governs the political advancement of these two social ideologies has produced untold misery, sacrifice, and the altering of many lives. Unfortunately, every social structure and every human being that exists in their particular social structure needs adversaries, and chaos to learn and grow. The continuance of human existence demands that we maintain a purpose for existing.

Our nation's leaders have attempted to coerce the citizens into believing that we have won the so-called cold war, and therefore our nation has achieved some great feat. And they truly expect us to accept that nonsense.

The communist and the feeble-minds that embrace the doctrine will always have a total disregard for peaceful coexistence. Accept as a crutch, the foundation of Communist social ideology is an infinite barrier that prevents them from having a meaningful relationship with any social structure governed by democratic principles. They are only hibernating, healing, waiting and watching. They have not abandoned their desire for world domination, and the abolishment of free will.

Clearly, the Soviet Union is in disarray and Russia appears to have troubles with terrorism and other social ills of their own, but they are not neutralized. As long as they have the enormous stockpile of Nuclear Weapons, they will always be a valid threat, if not an imminent one.

With the decline of a very aggressive Soviet nature, China has become the beast of the east; coiled like an aggressive deadly, social, and political viper, it is seeking the right opportunity to gobble up the remnants of democracy that manage to survive the overbearing offensive of terrorism. Relying totally upon our nation and its allies respect for the power of the Beast, Korea is a small, relatively insignificant social structure, except for their human factor, and there struggle to swim upstream to global recognition.

Since all animals crave freedom, no social structure that relies upon brutality or any other forms of intimidating restraints can dislodge it from the spirit of man. Embedded in the craving of all living beings, human or otherwise, is a natural desire for freedom. Therefore, the principles that nourish communism impede its ability to continue to function as it is practiced.

It may appear that Russia is little more than an annoyance, but it remains a world power. Its influence still slithers out from the bowels of demented souls, and promotes fear and barbarity to undermine the quest for a peaceful coexistence. A tentacle, a wicked social malignancy of its influence is the terrorism that it once supported and now imminently faces. This malignant social evil with lethal intentions has attached its fears to the essence of democracy and other lest notable social structures. The force that is required to curtail its amoral and aggressive nature spawns the elements for social progression.

While the principles of democracy permit a restricted version of the communist and other ideological dissidents to exist in our society, they denounce and plot to destroy the system of governing that allows them to fester and grow. Nurtured by the tentacles of democratic principles, they feed on our greed, our phobias, and even our democratic approach to handling their aggressive nature. Their actions pressure our government into moral and financial bankruptcy to slow their progress.

Still, the fundamental function of democracy must not be altered, are changed to combat communism or terrorism; for, it is a system of governing that allows the human spirit to flourish. The evolutionary progression of humanity is depending on its continuation.

The individuals and nations that seek to alter our social structure from within are an imminent threat. But their commitment to their goal is an even greater threat to the societies that are still within the primary stages of democratic governing.

If we allow these threats to exist unchallenged in the world's communities, democracy will eventually become isolated, and nurtured only by societies strong, and committed enough to repel the challenges.

I do not believe that America will ever completely abandon our way of life. However, democracy for all its intents and purposes has already entered into a state retrogression. Still, we are, and we will always remain a nation of free people, even beyond the ultimate reality of total destruction. But when the sum total of our struggle with terrorism is weighed, the essence of democracy will be severally altered.

Because we are a free society, democracy appears to have an element of weakness and vulnerability. That weakness is the essence of freedom, and it will always exist. Still, it would be unthinkably foolish, and dangerous for our adversaries to overestimate their ridiculous illusions that our nation will not repel any challenge.

In a country governed by a dictator or communism, there is a need for direct control. A dictator's fanatic actions are beyond scrutiny. In comparison, I will graciously admit that the nature of democracy exposes its inborn weaknesses.

Fortunately, the strength of our nation does not rely upon intimidation and brutality. It promises instead, that its social structure will allow the human spirit to flourish within the boundaries of our moral and social laws, and occasionally beyond them.

We have taken giant strides to become a greater, more united nation than we were. We must not let greed; senseless bigotry, shattered hopes and dreams propel our progress into a state of stagnation.

Removing the ghosts of past amoral idealism is essential to determining our survival of the challenges. We must embrace and protect our democratic principles, and our ability to function as a unit, and the rejuvenating of our patriotic spirit assures maximum effort. These principles fashioned the greatness of our nation.

A confrontation with our adversaries always appears imminent. But I do not honestly believe that barbaric or suicidal as our adversaries often appear, they are going to seriously hinder the progression of democracy to a position that time and decent political representation cannot repair. It is very difficult to consider that any nation or any group that represent any nation would risk the complete annihilation of humanity, just to display to the world that they are a power, or represent a power to be reckoned with.

When respect for America, and its values declined in the world's communities, our influence stagnated, and retarded the effectiveness of our unlimited power. Yet, wounded as we are, we shall rise to the occasion.

Crutches

THE SOCIAL POSITION OF THE bulk of the black race encourages a large sum of black people to settle on the generalization that our dark skin automatically diminishes our intellectual capabilities. Accepting the lowing of any standards so that we can participate, confirm that we do not have the will to compete.

The determining factors for social competition should be an individual's skills, behavior and their intellectual ability, not their ethnic heritage. I understand that blacks and other minorities are most often not playing on a level field, but playing on a level social field is not the relevant factor that hinders us.

The principles that nourish the process of learning are parental involvement, environment, desire, and the mental health of an individual. The color of one's skin is not important to the process. Still, if black people expect to compete, we must make every effort to learn and disprove the ridiculous generalization that blacks are inferior and hopelessly intellectually incompetent.

The continual erosion of moral values, concepts, and self-worth has victimized, deprived, and demoralized a large sum of our society, but particularly the black society. Because of the black race's seemly inability to employ, and maintain these standards that I mentioned, we are still in pursuit of the elusive recognition of total equality. Therefore, the bias judgmental, eyeballs of the established social hierarchy continues to focus on us.

Of course, there are other reasons why we still have not broken through the barriers that impede our social progress as a race. However, those that I mentioned previously appear to cause stagnation and hopelessness in black people more than it does any other group.

To confuse the obvious, which is our seemly inability to reach the social position of the white race, we rely much too often upon excuses that are no longer within the realm of progressive, social validity. We allow these excuses to camouflage the true explanation for our inability.

In order to compete successfully, we must demonstrate that we can compete with anyone. We must not sacrifice our self-esteem by embracing the lowering of any standards to compensate for our incompetence. When we allow other people to generalize that we are too stupid to learn, and compete on their academic level, we reinforce their claim to dominion over us. They are not going to consider that for some of us it is an infinite struggle just to exist in our environment, or the social obstacles that imminently threatened to overwhelm and demoralize our lives everyday. The mere fact that they have social dominance, and believe that they are dominant intellectually, is enough to claim superiority.

To upgrade our race's education and skills, black adults, whether we are parents or not, must have a greater influence on our children's social behavior, and academic excellence. If all our kids ever see is a crack head, or some person too lazy to flush the toilet, their perception of life does not have a very good beginning. We need to stop complaining about the difference in schools, and escort our kids to the neighborhood library. They must learn that 1+1=2 and that rap singers and pro athletes are not necessarily good role models. We must generate an inkling of pride for our black leaders, our race, and ourselves. We cannot allow anyone to sabotage the contributions of black people, or generalize our behavior, and intellectual abilities, because of the color of our skin, or the conduct of a few.

Of all our social constraints, the most confining and distracting to black people's social progression is poverty. An overwhelming percentage of us exist seemly without hope behind this obstacle. Although this obstacle appears to be almost impassable, we can overcome it if we do not allow ourselves to accept it. Poverty will not succumb to large sums of government assistance. If we do not adjust our attitudes, and our will to be resolute, government assistance can only enhanced our tolerance of the barriers that confines us.

The color of our skin and the seemly immovability of the social barriers are truly unimportant. If we apply ourselves as individuals, as a race we will gradually elevate to an acceptable level of intellectual competence. Only then will we be able to remove the tentacles of social bondage, and disprove the generalizations.

Poverty and low self-esteems have forced an enormous portion of black people to accept certain social essentials designed to aid the needy. I understand the poor and underprivileged individuals' needs for assistance, but if we are not cautious, social assistance can easily impede or destroy our abilities. It can also retard our determinations, and desires to be intellectually competent, and socially independent.

Generations of blacks continue to grow up in a limited social environment. Poverty and our dependence upon government assistance, more often than not, determine the quality of our meager existence. We appear to be hopelessly preconditioned to rely upon these crutches

The crutches and excuses will always be available to us. Past abuses, poverty, and government assistance are just a few. It is time for us to rid ourselves of them; for, they have worn thin from our dependency.

Justice and the Black Man

FROM THE BEGINNING OF BLACK peoples' unfortunate encounter with white people, we have been unjustly abuse. Our bodies, our souls, and our very existence were violated, and subdued by some of the lowest forms of inhumane justice.

In a fanatic attempt to suffocate the spirit of black people, some white people displayed, and still display their diabolic interpretation of justice. The written and unwritten laws thoroughly distorted the definition of fairness; therefore, becoming a lawful vehicle to persecute black people.

Justice was often used as an exhibition of absolute power. The apparent progress of our social structure may give an appearance of equality, but an enormous sum of black people are still helpless recipients of a dominant, white society's unscrupulous perceptions of right and wrong, justice and injustice.

The constitutional laws of our nation were created to govern and protect its citizens, but there was a time that we were recognized as citizens, therefore the laws were not functionally beneficial to black people. Because in the hearts of the social dominating people, we were considered to be second-classed, or none citizens, and there were no laws written for us. The inconsistency of the laws existed because some whites believed that because they had social dominion, justice and injustice were matters of individual will, or self-indulgence.

The constitutional explanations of Justice in our society suggest that the laws were created to be humanely fair. Still, in the continuing relationship between the law and black people, justice has always been blind, swift, and much too often enforced to the limits of its power.

Heroes

What make some people heroes?

Some would say that they are just fools.

Others would say that they are stupid people,

Who obviously loss their cool.

When individuals become heroes,

They forget about themselves,

And for a moment in their lives,

They conquer the fear of death.

Poverty

Poverty is a silent death. The poor are like puppets, struggling to scale the walls of a seemly inescapable existence of sorrow; clinging to our dwindling faith that there will be a better tomorrow.

We cry, we wait and some of us pray, until God send the angel of death to take us away.

Friendship

You should be proud to have a friend to help you every now and then.

Being alone and cannot get any help is the hardest thing for an individual to accept.

Friends are people who share with one another.

They are individuals that respect each other.

Tribute to Grandmothers

Thank God, for all the grandmothers that he has blessed us with.

They seem much better than mothers, and lots more fun to be with.

They are filled with so much kindness and love, and always so eager to spoil.

They let you gorge on delicious goodies that make you somewhat loyal.

They allow you to get away with murder, not many mothers would.

They sit in their rocking chairs, turn their heads, and pretend that they didn't see you do it.

Grandmothers are special, because they give young hearts such a lift.

God must have loaned them to us as one of his greatest gifts.

Haven of Solitude

The cool, wind blew its summer breeze

That whispered softly through the old oak trees.

The old folks gathered around in their chairs,

And told their tales of far gone years.

The church bell tolled for each hour of the day.

For some, it told the hour, for others, it was time to pray.

I lived in a haven of solitude, in times that were very hard.

I was a long way from heaven, but I felt close to God.

The Dreamer

To avoid, endure, or defeated the obstacles along the highways and byways of life requires an understanding of your dreams, faith, desires, and limitation. Understanding will improve your ability to survive and prosper. Very little that happens by chance increases the prosperity of anyone. You must plan the route that you are going to follow in your life to achieve your perception of success and the enjoyment of that success.

One of man's greatest traits is our ability to dream and contrive. From the dreams of humanity new worlds were discovered and kingdoms were either conquered or they conquered.

The unveiling and the application of an individual's dreams furnish the motivation for man's assault on new frontiers. When an individual or a society ceases to dream, stagnation will occur, and the fundamental function of the individual or the society will eventually perish.

True Beauty and Ugliness

A combination of grace and charm that is pleasing to the eye or gratifying to the esthetic senses is the definition of beauty. We consider ugliness as repelling and displeasing.

Unfortunately, the factor that primarily influences our recognition of beauty and ugliness is the labor of our perception. But because of hasty generalization, we do not allow ourselves enough time to see the true beauty or ugliness of anyone or anything.

True beauty is an unpolluted entity in the human soul. To discover it in an individual or a thing, we must take into account the fundamental functioning of that individual or thing before we assess our opinions.

Social conditioned response, individual desires, pleasures, and emotions have conditioned us to be attracted to anyone or anything that we consider beautiful, and repel that in which we cannot see beauty.

The outer appearance of an individual or thing does not indicate or deny the true beauty or ugliness of that individual or thing.

Someone conjured up the statement that beauty is skin deep and ugliness is to the bone. This is an untrue statement, because both true beauty and ugliness are functions of the soul, and the fundamental function of a thing. It has also been said that beauty is in the eyes of the beholder. This is true, but if the soul of the beholder is impatient and insensitive, they will be unable to recognize true beauty wherever it exists.

Collision Course with God

Humanity is approaching the climax of our existence.

Uncaring, we maintain a steady pace.

We are on a collision course with God,

That could destroy the human race.

We have an arsenal of destructive bombs,

And smart, computer machines.

Unfortunately, we have forgotten that what is most important,

Is that we love our fellow human beings.

We are stumbling down the avenues of destruction,

And that is to say the least.

Among all the formulas that we possess,

Is there not one for peace?

The people of the world must have a great change in our hearts,

In order to evade our collision course with God.

Black Beauty

Black women are beautiful.

They are such lovely sights to see.

Oh, how I wished almighty God

Had created them all for me.

At times, they are kind and good,

Like the gentleness of a drizzling rain,

But when they show their evil side,

They roar like a hurricane.

A mistreated black woman

Is the most unpredictable female alive.

It can be like stumbling naked,

Into a thousand angry beehives.

Happy Feelings

Like a child, I dance up and down.

My feet barely touch the ground.

I smile, laugh and sing,

To show the world what happiness can bring.

I try to share my pleasure with the whole, wide world,

With my mother, father and my girl.

My eyes are glowing but no tears are there.

You can see the light in them from almost anywhere.

Happy feelings are what I feel,

And I would like to show the world that my happiness is for real.

Bondage

The black male must become a proud black man.

We must emerge from the shadows and take our stand.

Are we to live in social captivity because of the pigments in our skin?

Socially caged by the white man who says "Hi friend."

Black people have endured bondage for centuries.

That is enough for me.

When God created the human race, he created us all to be free.

Must we destroy the white man in order to make him pay?

Kill him-kill the white man, is that what God would say?

He created man, as he sat on his throne above.

He gave his children a planet.

Did he forget to give us love?

Greatness

Greatness is a product of an individual's dreams.

Our worth is measured by the joy that we bring.

We may be rich or poor; the spoils of our lives

May be more than we can endure.

So, greatness is not measured in dollars and cents,

Or the things that we can buy.

But by the joy and love we bring to others before we die.

The Ghetto

An invisible wall, so resolute and confining,

A nightmare, from which there seems to be no escape.

Children cry silently while they lie awake.

The soft, shuffle of tiny bare feet; rumblings in the lining of small,

Black bellies, ice water in the refrigerator, peanut butter and jelly.

Teenage moms cry in fear; will the welfare feed their children this year?

Pimps and whores on the corners;

Rats, roaches, and broken down shacks,

Dope fiends wrestle with the monkeys on their backs.

The thundering roar of an instrument of death;

The blood curdling sounds of screaming sirens,

A young black's blood flows like water down a stream.

A ghetto mother grieves.

A nightmare—shattered dreams.

The Power of Mr. C

Something just occurred to me.

I was possessed by the power of Mr. C.

It can kill the body and destroy the mind.

It has humbled the best and the worst of us.

It may eventually destroy humankind.

It possesses and destroys our poor sisters and brothers.

It has brought down teachers, doctors, lawyers and others.

Mesmerized by the tiny rock so white, it confuses one's perceptions of wrong and right.

So many souls have been lost, but who is keeping score?

Crack has turned many good women into whores.

If you hitch a ride to that dead-end road, you had better ride well,

Because your destination my friends is straight to hell.

A Friend of Mine

I saw a friend of mine the other day climbing gracefully up a tree.

He was somewhat busy, but took time out to notice me.

He is just a little fellow that people call a squirrel.

I would not trade our friendship for anything in the world.

Early every morning he sits on my windowsill.

When I look out to see him there, God only knows the love that I feel.

The squirrel is such a friendly animal, so agile and free.

When I die and re-incarnate, a squirrel, I would like to be.

Universal Madness

Have the whole damn world gone mad? Have we reached the revelation of our existence? We have almost succeeded in disrupting the natural balance of life on our planet, and though we have contaminated our environments, the complex functions of God's creation continue. Fortunately, we will crash head on with God before we reach the point of total destruction.

Carelessly, we ignore the clear evidence that reveal the sinister imperfections of our behavior. These flaws may ultimately determine the destiny of all life.

We claim to be human, but we behave like demons, coerced by the lurking presence of evil. Our just rewards shall be death-the extermination of all life.

Oh God, have thou forsaken us?

My Shadow and Me

Everyday at dawn, my shadow and I go outside to greet the morning sun.

We are united, yet separate, friends from birth to the tomb.

My shadow has always been my companion, even in my mother's womb.

When the day is done, the darkness devours the sun.

My shadow creeps back inside my soul; once again, I am whole.

Before I lay me down to sleep, I kneel beside my bed to pray that shadow and I will greet the dawning of another day.

Sinner in Purgatory

God, must this be my destiny, to flutter on the winds of time-lost for eternity; engulfed in the infiniteness of time and space; waiting to be judge in that final court, and then cast down into the deepest bowels of hell?

Suspended in a state of unending torment, my existence is far beyond any mortal expectation. From the portal between mortal existence and infinity, the essence of that mortal journey spirals toward me. If this is not hell, then the vengeance of the devil must be an unbearable existence.

The Eagle's Claw

A tiny thread supports the balance of human existence.

Hordes of souls silently await their destiny.

A single voice echoes, "I shall make the world free!"

A relentless challenge from the east;

An eagle's claw blocks its path.

Billions of souls wait to see what power the eagle's claw may be.

No Escape

An individual labors throughout the day.

The weight of the world is upon their chest.

They long for it all to end.

In the wee hours of the night, while they lie in silent slumber,

They are confronted by events that have been absorbed into their subconscious,

And are flowing unrelentingly into their view.

Angel of Death

No human being is better than any others,

We are all sisters and brothers.

It is unimportant what color we are, or whether we are rich or poor,

Because when we die and leave this place, to dust we will all go.

Almighty God created us in the image of himself,

And it does not matter who we are, we will all face the angel of death.

Black Oppression

THE BLACK RACE IS STILL oppressed. Even with the great strides, and social advancements of a few, a very large number of us are almost hopelessly bound by the mental and social chains that continue to hold us enslaved.

The links of the chains have weakened because of the unselfish efforts of a select group, a chosen few, who gave the full measure of their devotion to our struggle. Yet, the relentless might of oppression remains an uncompromising factor in our lives. It is not that we are not capable of removing the chains, but too many years of poverty, illiteracy, and social aggravation have created an atmosphere of acceptance.

If the black race is ever going to be truly equal, we must demonstrate that we can achieve an acceptable standard of intellectual competence and pride. Still misled by the slogan, black is beautiful, some of us unfortunately believe that blackness possesses some sort of magical charm that automatically provides us with the tools to exist in our complex society. The slogan was only an attempt to instill in us a measure of racial pride, and self-confidence.

Through education and awareness, not black beauty, the higher social level that we seek is within reach. Social domination and oppression exist on that level. If our race is going to have a successful campaign, not only must we have educated, and dedicated black leaders, but also an educated and aware black society.

A few us still choose to demonstrate our frustration with oppression by engaging in violence and retribution. It appears that in our opinion, the only means for our continual existence is to exterminate the oppressors, and burn our neighborhoods.

Once a crowd or a group becomes a mob, the fuel that ignited the flame is never truly the motivating factor that sustains it. Right or wrong, while behaving like a horde of soulless beast, we use the event that created the mob as an excuse to create havoc. We have taken what were once demonstrations against social injustices and turned them into convincing negative floor shows, while becoming the mob that we feared and hated.

The destruction and burning of our neighborhoods and the uncontrolled violence creates negative generalizations in the news medial, and reinforces the minds and hearts of those who are already bias. It lends a degree of support for those who suggest that these actions are the limit of black peoples' social capabilities.

This is an irrational tactic, and therefore, unacceptable. In the first place, it just does not make sense to wreck havoc on your own neighborhood. But to behave violently against any human being, group or race, for any purpose, excluding total self-preservation cannot be the answer. The fragile balance of our social structure will not withstand the destructive potential of that type of social disruption. Our nation cannot survive the catastrophe end.

To avoid provoking the wrath of the majority's retaliation there are only a few rational and effective paths that black people can travel. We must travel the path of a more educated race of people. Simply put, we must limit the jitterbugging and learn to read. We must provide a united effort and generate a decent amount of respect for each other. In addition, at least a tidbit of common sense and morality must govern the contents of our character. Above all, some white people associate the behavior of black people with applied logic's more frequent used fallacy; they generalize that the behavior of the sum of its parts is parallel to the character of the whole.

The Edge of Rage

Two bare feet and kinky hair, a roaring in the lining of his small, black belly.

For him, black is not beautiful, but a chocolate colored hell;

A grim reality of a world in which it seems he has no place.

Suffering, hunger and pain, so small is he to endure.

If he should survive to become a man, filled with bitterness a thousand-fold; Too long has his heart been dead;

Too long has he felt the hellish fury of his oppressors

That still threatens to devour him.

The dead weight of the world is upon him,

And he must survive in a society where the color of love is green.

Don't Look Down on Me

Don't look down on me black brother, you came from the ghetto too.

I may be ragged, black and poor, but that is nothing new to you.

Don't look down on me.

Who do you think you are?

Do you think that you are better than I am, because you drive a fancy car?

You used to live in the ghetto.

I remember you well.

The reason you drive out of your way

Is to keep from passing through this hell.

Every since you made your great escape, your life has not been the same.

Hurrah for you, I am glad that you overcame.

Someday, I may scale the walls of poverty, and if my life should change,

I will not forget the people that I leave, in the ghetto, from whence I came.

Brothers Underneath

Just beneath the thin layers of our dark, brown skin,

Is indisputable evidence that all humankind is kin.

That is where the color stops, and the human being began.

Just beneath our dark, brown skin is no different from any other man.

Elements of Life

Love, hate, life and death, joy and sorrow;

Without these basic elements, there would be no tomorrow.

When Adam sinned in the Garden of Eden,

God issued a solemn promise,

That there would be life, and death, until the end of time among us.

Love, hate, life and death, joy and sorrow,

Are things that man must bare

We might as well be satisfied,

Because they are not going anywhere.

A Smile

Every human being should make an effort every once and awhile,

To remove the frowns on their faces, and replace them with a smile.

Any day in our lives may be up or down,

But it does not cost anymore to smile, than it does to frown.

Black Values

A FEW CENTURIES AGO, BLACK people were abducted, and used as slaves in America. In our native country, our ethics and values were unique for our environmental existence. When we were forced to adapt to the new environment, we were stripped of our dignity, values and pride. Because the values of the new social structure were not available to us, precious remnants of our identity dripped from our brows, until our worn bodies fertilized the "Master's" soil.

After a few centuries of blatant, fanatic, inhuman oppression, certain parties of society decided that the abolishment of slavery was a key issue in the nation's attempt to remain united and grow.

Thousands of human beings suffered and died to allow us to taste the sweet nectar of that freedom. Despite all of the carnage and suffering, we were still not free. We had been deprived of freedom to long; therefore, the word had no substance.

Because the knowledge that we so desperately needed to survive in a society still bitter and hostile was unavailable to us, we remained stagnant, while clinging to mere existence. In spite of that, as generations of blacks evolved and progressed, we gradually learned to hold our heads high, and gaze into the eyes of our oppressors.

As the pursuit of knowledge became important to some of us, poverty and bigotry wrapped their tentacles around the majority us, and held us in check. Eventually, a few courageous blacks demanded freedom throughout our society. From the efforts of those brave, heroic individuals, and sympathetic whites, we became a race with limited freedom.

The cry for freedom slowly slithered into the bosom of time, and a new value took its place. From the souls of black people with limited freedom, an outcry for equality echoed.

Muddy Mississippi

I stood on the bank of old muddy, early one summer day,

And watched the speed of its currents, as they passed my way.

I thought of the lives that the river had claimed,

In the years that had passed and gone.

In sorrow, I imagined the agony of the souls that called old muddy home.

When Gabriel blows his trumpet, the bodies in old muddy will float,

And never again will it flow down another human's throat.

Nobody

I stood in the midst of a multitude of people, yet I was alone.

An insignificant individual, stripped of my dignity,

Everything that I owned was gone.

My soul whimpered, to be touched and caressed,

But no one heard its plea.

I stood alone, just me, just me.

Shacks in the Back

Too many years we slaved for the white folks.

We were always doing this or that.

While they lived in the houses on the hills,

We lived in the shacks in the backs.

We scrubbed their floors, cleaned their dishes,

And washed their dirty drawers.

We worked ourselves damn near to death,

For yah suh, oh yah suh boss.

Maybe we cannot stop white people from telling us this and that.

Then let us go live in the houses on the hills,

And damn the shacks in the backs.

Clothes Do Not Make a Man.

When I was just a little fellow with ragged clothes, and feet so bare,

I swore to God that someday,

I would have clothes like those that the white folks wear.

I would stroll around, all pure and clean,

With my nose up in the air.

I would do all the things that they were doing,

And some that they did not dare.

But when I grew older and wiser, and my feet were longer in the sand,

I discovered that clothes did not make a man.

The Struggle

A large portion of the black race is still struggling through a hell of an existence. Enslaved in the grips of poverty; bound and gagged by the boundaries of the pigments in our skin. Reluctantly, we struggle mentally and physically, reaching out with almost futile, but reckless abandon.

It is only our desire to survive; to exist that keeps us from tumbling into the bowels of hell.

Life Can Be a Wicked Curse

People struggle through life and its horrible pains.

We beg for mercy, but the pains remain,

Like a spilled soda or a mustard stain.

Sometimes, we are up, and sometimes down.

We must not let life keep us on the ground.

Sometimes life gets better; sometimes it gets worst.

Often, it can be a nightmare, or a wicked curse.

Don't Give Up

If you fall in defeat, do not give up.

Scramble to your feet, you still might have luck.

The power of the mind can conquer all things,

And separate one's reality from their dreams.

The word failure is unreal.

Do not be afraid, it is just something that you feel.

Organize your efforts; do your very best.

When your chance comes, you may be better than the rest.

The Prey and the Predator

HUMANITY'S STRUGGLE TO UNRAVEL THE mysteries of human behavior failed because we could not generate an understanding of its randomness. Our refusal to acknowledge that our fundamental instincts govern our behavior prevents us from achieving that understanding.

If we do not accept the fact that we are primarily animals, not just in a zoological arrangement sense, but also by the display of our behavior, we will never understand. When we think of animals, we naturally assume that we are referring to species that are beneath the zoological arrangement of man. But if we compared our behavior with the behavior of other animals, particularly primates, the only rational conclusion is that as complex as we are, we are just another species of animals.

The primary biological device that supports our claim to being human is that we have a soul. The soul is an entity that houses a spirit. It is this spirit from which God created us in his likeness. It elevates us above the remainder of the animal kingdom. But simply because we have a spirit and other abilities that are far beyond those of any other species of animals, do not exclude the fact that we were animals in the beginning, and we still are, but not the descendants of apes, or any other species.

Our large, complex brain and the structure of our biological life support system provide us with the ability to be at the top of the food chain. It is called having dominion. Because we have this ability to dominate the remainder of the animal kingdom, we challenge any notion that we could possibly be anything less than human.

Sure, our schools teaches us that man is an animal, but we are not instructed on how the partitioning of our souls will determine whether our behavior will be governed by our basic instincts, or our faith and obedience to God, our creator.

Because we have the ability and the natural desire to dominate other species, we cannot disassociate these cravings with regard to our own species. Almost without effort, we are compelled to dominate the weaker of the human animal.

A solid moral foundation, and a genuine desire to surrender ourselves to the principles in the Holy Scriptures, is the only vehicle that can possibly impede the effectiveness of our natural behavioral influence.

Power, greed, idolatry worship, and all the other unrighteous, ungodly elements are vehicles of Satan that corrupts our ability to behave like the human beings created in the likeness of God, rather than animals governed by natural instincts.

Our ability to adapt, to sustain, and socially evolve is sufficiently explained in Darwin's theories of evolution. By no means do I agree that man evolve from some other species, but the survival of the fittest and natural selection are principles that govern the entire animal kingdom, and the social evolution of the human race. These natural principles dictate our social behavioral responses. Unfortunately, the ability and the desire to have absolute power are necessary components to the progression of human social development. The social evolution of the human race has always depended upon adversity, calamities, and social catastrophes to learn, and adjust for continuous growth.

Modern man has declared himself civilized; yet we constantly demonstrate our appetite for absolute power and a total disregard for our own species by conquering, enslaving and destroying each other. So then, we are no less predatorily than any other predator. How do we then determine who is civilized and who is not? In addition, how are we to determine the degree of our civilization?

The answers to these questions are very simple. First of all, civilization is not a social condition that is absolute. It is considered to be the humane behavior and intellectual advancements of people in a particular environment that usually determines the degree of civilization in that particular environment.

Enormous portions of humanity have assembled our natural habitats into large cities, towns, and communities. These habitats consist of mortar, brick, concrete, and all of the other elements that we use to sustain and improve our existence. These are our concrete jungles. We assume that we are more civilized than people living in undeveloped areas because we live in these concrete environments, and supposedly, our technological advancements has elevated us to a higher level than our fellow human beings.

In the near future, we will assemble outposts in space, and it is probable that some of us will eventually live there. We will also build cities beneath the world's oceans. Yet, regardless of where we exist, only our faith in the living God can elevate us beyond the laws that govern our natural instincts.

If an individual does not possess the moral fiber to aid them in controlling the behavioral response of environmental and social evolutionary conditioning, the part of the individual's soul that make them human will be greatly diminished.

Morals have their limits in human behavioral response to environmental stimuli. But if they are not a functioning part of our souls, the soul will rely upon its natural instincts. These instincts will not allow us to behave humanly, but like the predators and scavengers of other species.

The survival of the fittest is a logical, but complex law, when applied to the behavioral functioning of human beings. Because we do not understand the relationship between human behavior and this law, we dismiss the fact that it truly governs our natural, behavioral responses.

Nations are conquered, or they conquer. The destruction and assimilation of social structures, and cultures, and the enslavement of people because they are not as strong as their enemies are, can be attributed to this law. Because most of us do not eat each other, do not suggest that our predacious intentions are not governed by the same natural instincts as the predators of other species.

Since we have no natural enemies other than each other, nature's wrath, wars, the mass slaughter of human beings, genocide, and ethnic cleansing are tools. They function as an aid to control the human population, just as other predators prey on the vulnerability of the weak to keep a particular species healthy.

Death is the destiny of all living things. Humans like other predators are primordially programmed to aid nature in the maintenance of our species. To make us appear civilized we have social laws to minimize the destructive potential of our predacious intentions. All predatory animals kill for food and self-preservation. Sadly, man also kills for pleasure, dominion over other men, and other reasons, motivated by our flaws and weaknesses.

Wars and conflicts are nature's masquerades. We are conditioned to believe that they are struggles over territory, or social ideology, but they are truly nature's maintenance tools.

The birth rate in the nations that are least capable of sustaining their population has increased enormously. The global life expectancy has also increased tremendously. Our planet houses six billion or more people. In order for the human race to have a quality existence in the future, and not totally demolish the existence of other species, we will have to continue to manufacture more wars, conflicts, diseases, and other means of population control.

Our continuing search for new frontiers in space for the sake of knowledge, and wonderment is enlightening, but we cannot feed the population of our planet with rocks from Mars and Jupiter. We consume enormous sums of much needed wealth on fruitless adventures into space primarily for the sake of adventure and competition.

A society can construct the most elaborate system of mass destruction, and self-defense, but every social structure is in danger, when a greater portion of humanity is starving. However, it really does not matter what we do; world wars, ethnic cleansing, conflicts, the predatory, social behavior of man, sickness and plagues, and natural disasters are all nature's maintenance tools used to thin the horde.

If all of the social structures of the human race evolved into a united, global community, as some has prophesied, and if we began to love each other; thinking alike, and peacefully coexisting, we will have achieved the prophecy of the Bible, and we will cease to exist.

The Classification of Human Beings

MAN IS ONE OF MANY social animals. We tend to group ourselves according to our race, bloodlines, and economic statues. The known history of humanity will show that even beyond race and bloodlines, people have always had a need to organize themselves into special categories and groups. The obvious question is whether the classification of people is necessary. Utilizing a tidbit of common sense will reveal that the rational answer is no.

In almost every wild or civilized environment of social animals, there are recognized social positions. These positions are usually determined by individual's ability to denominate other members of their natural habitats or environments who are less prepared to sustain themselves.

America's social structure and some others are partitioned into an assortment of classes. They range from high to low. In the more advanced democratic societies, the color of love has turn to green; therefore, economic status has become the primary parameter that determines the class positions.

Should an individual be labeled as low class, simply because they do not have money, or social position? Are they any less human than other human beings are? Do they not function in the same manner as those who senselessly claim their blood to be blue?

Individual social behavior should be the only factor that determines class position in a civilized social environment. The high economic status of an individual merely suggests that they can afford a more comfortable standard of existence. They are not special, more important, or righteous than anyone else is. It is not the so-called purity of an individual's blood, or the color of their skin, nor their economic status, that is relevant to the classification of people.

The black race has always associated the classification of people with racism and bigotry. We view it as a vehicle of social oppression. Because we are still oppressed citizens in America, we consider classification as a social condition that is unique to us.However, there have always been oppressed people. The archives of human history will show that humans have always had a natural desire to oppress other humans by declaring ourselves supreme, or more human than a selected group. It tells of African tribes who enslaved their rivals, and of emperors, kings and queens of other races who enslaved members of their race.

Classification and Oppression are social malignancies, nurtured by the appetite for power and domination. They disrupt the delicate balance of coexisting, and hinder our ability to respect each other.

As far as the black race is concerned, the pigments in our skin just happen to be dark. In most cases, based sorely on that fact, some white people still campaigns to maintain the shallow illusion of racial superiority. They suggest that blackness is a trait that is associated with inferior humans, and have no claim to totally equality. However, people with pale skin risk their lives, while spending billions of dollars annually to darken their skin. Yet, they say that it is inferior to have dark skin, or to be an offspring of dark skin ancestry. Apparently, skin tone is not the absolute issue. The reference to our dark skin and the negative name-calling is primarily frightened individuals or groups' efforts to conceal their lack of tolerance, their fears and jealousy.

Skin color has nothing to do with the arrangement of an individual's concepts, or the contents of their character. These are the only relevant characteristics for equality.

In the beginning, God created a male and a female. Common sense would suggest that both of the individuals would possess the same color of skin. If he had wanted anyone to claim superiority because of the color of their skin, would he not have mentioned it?

People are nothing more than grains of sand in a desert of humanity. We are unique, individual particles endowed with many colors, sizes, shapes, and economic statuses. Still, we all contribute equally to the formation of the desert.

Last Rights

I remember when my mind was so unstable.

I wanted to be killed, but no one would do me the favor.

I lied, stole and did odd jobs to get my drugs.

My soul was mortally wounded.

I could not feel a thing.

I lived each day for the mean, mean green.

Crack had sabotaged my life.

I did not realize that I was sick,

Until I sold my car for a ten-dollar hit.

I tried over, and over again to change.

In the end, the results were always the same.

Now, I am in the midst of a spiritual warfare.

I am fighting things that are unseen, transparent and unclear.

The energy that envelops me regulates my thoughts.

It constantly reminds me of my failures and faults.

There is always something good or bad,

Shoving and shifting me from happy to sad.

My hopes and dreams are relentless episodes of pain.

With one foot in hell, I am almost insane.

Sometimes, I scream from the bowels of insanity.

No one seems to hear my cry.

The battle continues but I will not lie down and die.

Self-destruction

The black man is his own worst enemy,

Still, we call each other brother.

We seem to take great pleasure in annihilating each other.

We rape our females, be they young or old.

We think that pimping our black women is the ultimate goal.

If we do not develop some morals, and arrange the contents of our character,

We will go on destroying each other.

The skin heads and Ku Klux Klan won't have to.

Combating Racism

Once we could see, taste and feel the awesome might of a dominant, and prejudice, white society. However, over a period of a few decades or so, human rights have won a decent share of its scrimmages with the malignancies that we call prejudice and bigotry, but the war continues.

The efforts of a special group of black and white people partially disrupted the effectiveness of the two social malignancies. They were forced reluctantly back into the dark, caverns of the individuals' souls. When the malignancies bonded with the feeble emotions housed in the septic tank that we call the soul, they mutated and fester, because they did not recede of their own free will. If an individual's soul is tainted by the malignancies for any moderate period of time, they are usually embedded to deep to be removed.

The effort to neutralize prejudice and bigotry before it flushes the tender emotion from the soul must begin in our homes with the teaching of our children. We must train them while their souls are fresh to respect the dignity and the rights of others. This respect should not be given because of the color of an individual's skin, their social position, or economic status, but because they are human beings. If we can get our children to accept this concept, we can possibly curtail the malignancies.

Female Equality

If I could stand before the world, a story I would tell,

Of how God created the heavens and the earth,

And discovered that he had done well.

Then to his majestic mind came such a wonderful thought,

"A man I'll create," he said, "One that can walk and talk."

He reached down, filled his hands with clay, and fashioned a man so bold.

He breathed the breath of life in him, and gave man a soul.

Now man was lonely in the world, as plainly God could see,

So he created a woman to keep him company.

Why God created a woman is no mystery,

And though, he created her last, he created her equality.

Moonlight Over the Mountain

There is a moonlit night over the mountain.

The stars are shining bright above.

God made the moon for lovers.

He made the moonlight for love.

The moonlit night over the mountain,

Makes your heart feel light and free.

God made the moon for lovers,

And he made the moonlight for me.

Ku Klux Whites

When black people demanded freedom and equality,

They called it communism.

They beat the hell out of all they could,

And sent the rest to prison.

They bombed our churches, killed our children,

And cut out our brothers' hearts.

They assassinated our greatest leaders,

And called it the will of God.

There are still some whites that would like to kill us all,

Or send us off to some prison.

In Russia, they do the very same thing,

But they call that communism.

Born Free

America is the greatest nation on earth.

Freedom is an inheritance from an individual's day of birth.

The black man has been here hundreds of years,

Yet, the only thing that we have inherited is pain, sorrow and tears.

We fought, we cried, and some of us died,

But for some reason, God let the black man survive.

Religion and Moral Behavior

The alliance between religion and moral behavior is inseparable. I will explain their relationship in the process of molding a young individual's character.

Religion is the catalyst that launches the foundation for moral behavior. It is the principles written on the pages of the Bible that teach us how to behave and coexist with one another.

We must begin to teach these principles early in our young children lives. The only stage in human development that the character of an individual can be successfully molded is before their souls are tainted by the afflictions of human natural instinct and a contaminated social structure. Therefore, it is absolutely important that every young individual be introduced to the principles in the Bible as a vital component of their everyday existence.

It is the obligation of every parent to ensure that their children understand the advantages and the disadvantages of good and bad behavior. To successfully shape a young individual's character, a parent must teach the importance of good moral values, and social behavior. They must also live their lives in such away that the child will have an opportunity to learn from perception.

Discipline is absolutely the most important component to a child's ability to learn, and to their moral growth and sound behavior. A steady diet of it is necessary to a child's character. Regardless of a child's learning potential, you cannot teach them anything, if you are unable to command their attention and respect.

As adults, we often complain that the younger generations' values and social behavior have eroded considerably. And yes, it is apparent that our children are living their lives spiritually famished from the absence of the presence of God. They are also mentally and socially unbalanced because of the need for the parental guidance that we once called mother wit.

Our schools once played a vital role in helping to shape the social behavior of young people, but the introduction and advancement of child psychology limits their contribution. When we eliminated the paddle, and the piss elm limb, and install the scientific philosophy referred to as child psychology, we committed an irreversible mistake.

The word of God has also vanished not only from our schools, but our halls of justice, and every vehicle that could have a positive effect on our children. Still, we pretend that we are baffled by our kids' behavior.

As far as most black kids are concern, particular males, sending them to their rooms, or taking away their privileges will not control their behavior. A silent rage, fueled by the sum of all of their circumstances must be regulated in a large group of young black males. Only religion, morals, and discipline can cripple their aggressive nature.

High on Life`

I felt the wind caressing my face—

A moment of unimaginable bliss, as my mind orbited in space.

High on life and moving fast,

I was comforted by the memories of my not so distant past.

I inhaled the intoxicating sweetness of the gentle morning air.

Suddenly, I forgot that I was still standing there.

The birds were singing a song of love.

As they sang, the sky blossomed above.

I thanked God for the wonderful day.

I knew that it had to end, but I wished it would stay.

The lingering clouds slowly dispersed.

In awe, I watched as the heavens transformed into a wondrous blue.

The beauty of Mother Nature was unveiled with the morning dew.

Jack Frost sparkled on the grass.

Those were the wonderful things that make life last.

Racial Prejudices

PREJUDICES ARE NATURAL FLAWS IN human character. There are many variations that occupy the soul. We all have our preferences; therefore, no one is exempt from its destructive influences.

The definition of prejudice primarily states that it is a product of an irrational attitude, or hostility toward an individual, group or race. Because it demonstrates the unpredictability of human behavior, the word irrational seems to be the only reasonable explanation.

The existence of the black race was once reduced to the mere importance of jackasses, simple beast of labor. I experienced a brief period of time existing in such an environment. I thought that it would be easy for me to identify the mechanism that encourages the desire for dominion, hate, and indifference.

In a sincere effort to understand prejudice and bigotry, I tried to analyze my feelings toward other individuals who were racially, culturally, and otherwise different. Based purely on my feelings, I concluded that it was only our human biological flaws that control our irrational conduct, and influence prejudice and bigotry.

The survival of the fittest, dominion and natural selection are primary flaws embedded within human nature. All human beings have the ability to regard themselves as being better than other humans.

To understand human behavior, we must take into account the basic negative elements of human nature. These elements are greed, fear, jealousy, envy, pride, self-exaltation, and a natural craving for dominion over our fellowman. We appear to have an infinite reluctance to obtaining the basic understanding that is crucial to the development of social tolerance, and the lack of prejudice.

People are not born prejudice or bigots, but with the capacity to embrace it. As we grow, and our souls develop, we learn from social and environmental conditioning how to hate, and to crave dominion and feel supreme. If the soul of an individual is infected with these flaws for any moderate period of time, they will be imbedded to deep to be removed without divine intervention. The individual will also likely influence the souls of others. Hate has the ability to spread like an epidemic. When the soul is influenced by any of the negative elements of human character, the individual cannot function with any degree of reasoning.

Prejudice and bigotry is a functioning part of the soul, and its influence has no boundaries. So, it is my conclusion that racial prejudice and bigotry will never be eradicated. While they feed and fester on the feeble emotions that inhabit the soul, the social environments that nurture them, also encourage them. Ultimately, they develop many disguises, and eat away the part of the soul that governs not only an individual's moral stability, but also their ability to simply reason. Eventually, an abundance of unrestrained hate, fears, and misguided reasoning escape the soul's infected pit.

White Tyranny

Hey nigga, black boy, is an echo heard by black people,

Existing under the tyranny of white people with our ungodly fears.

I will not hate—I will not bare a grudge.

I will not trample them with my feet every time I get the urge.

For I know at the end of time there will be a judgment day,

And for everything they have done God will make them pay.

The Moral Decay
of America's Children

OUR NATION'S CHILDREN ARE ITS greatest resource. The parents watch helplessly, while they perish under the strain of becoming young adults in an aggressive and complex society. The overpowering gravity of peer pressure, and social competition has generated in them an enormous degree of recklessness. Much too often unbridled, their intellectual awareness has accelerated to the degree that they cannot wait to become adults. Because they do not allow themselves to gradually grow into adulthood, there is a tremendous probability that they will be mentally, socially, and morally unbalanced. Unbridled intellect usually disrupts spiritual, mental and moral balance.

Our society spends enormous sums of money and time searching for solutions to our children's rebellious behavior. While there are many factors that influence them, the most destructive of these factors are our unwillingness, or our inability to administer discipline.

As adults and parents of these young people, we often attempt to rid ourselves of the responsibility for their behavior by transferring the blame to other areas of society. We can discuss all of the other social elements that can influence a young individual's behavior, but if we do not factor in the importance of discipline, everything else becomes irrelevant. Discipline is as important to moral growth, as the proper consumption of nourishment is to their physical well being. However, there are a small percentage of young individuals who need less direct discipline. Yet, the creation of more prisons, and still there is an overcrowding, suggest that there is a constant deterioration of moral values, and social behavioral accountability in our society.

We should teach our children as soon as they have the ability to comprehend that there are significant differences between right and wrong. They must understand that there are social and moral laws, rules, and principles that they must follow, if they are going to have an opportunity to survive and prosper. It has become very difficult to install in a child's mind the consequences for disobedience. Since any form of discipline is associated with child abuse, many caring parents and adults allow other social devices to develop and control the behavior of their children. Instead of allowing the parents and the schools to discipline our children, the police, the prisons, and the finality of the grave have become surrogate parents.

There is a decline of the two-parent family. A child needs the love and the discipline that two parents can provide. However, two parents are not absolutely necessary, if an intimate relationship with God has been established. It is not impossible for a single parent to install in their children a solid moral foundation, but it is unlikely that they can enforce their standards with the limited amount of quality time that is usually associated with single parenthood. A child's most active vehicle for learning is perception. They can easily absorb any negative influence, if there is an absence of proper supervision.

Poverty is the most dehumanizing, and crippling factor that can totally dictate the behavior of any individual, and it appears to have a greater effect in our black society than any others. It produces an overwhelming degree of hopelessness, shattered dreams, and deceptions, while encouraging the desire to strike out at anyone, or anything.

Young impoverished individuals are more susceptible to the woes of poverty than their older counterparts are. They exist behind a seemly impregnable window that allows them to observe all of the marvelous bounties that our society has to offer, but not to possess them. They are more likely to succumb to bitterness, despair and rebellion.

Our young people are also influence by the characters of unscrupulous television programs, video games and movies. Because of the absence of real role models or proper supervision, they idolize these characters as heroes and role models. Kids have been mimicking their heroes and embracing them as role models for as long as the term has existed.

Fortunately, the characters of the past were far less violent and convincing than today's bunch. Still, we took our B.B guns and cap pistols into the woods, and played cowboys and Indians.

Our kids can easily associate the movies and their video games to the relentless display of violence in our modern society, and the global community as a whole, where these progressive technologies exist. These games and movies by the exhibition of their violent content often influence, and enhance the natural predatory instincts of young people. Because the young souls are usually morally and spiritually undeveloped, perception is the primary source that nurtures them.

Drugs and alcohol are too abundant and accessible, and the immoral antics of pornography rob the kids of their innocence. Because our society tolerates these elements, they are not going to be easy to remove. Therefore, as parents and adults, our only recourse is to establish a solid relationship with God and our children. The relationship between God, parent, and child will serve as an insulator, or at the very least provide a format for the child's moral growth. The moral growth of an individual can only be cultivated and strengthened, while the individual is within the disciplinary stages of physical, spiritual, and mental growth.

The complex functioning of our society offers many varieties of diversions that can ravish the souls of the morally bankrupt, undisciplined young individuals. These individuals often find themselves engaged in a bitter struggle with society, and their own confused ideas concerning proper social behavior.

The adults and parents are always searching for some place to lay the blame, rather than to admit to the imperfection in our own character, and role model abilities. Until we are prepared to demonstrate some role model responsibilities, and examine the social dilemmas with a greater degree of rational scrutiny, our children, our society, and even our global communities will continue to suffer.

On the pages of my Bible, it says that each new generation would become weaker and wiser. The prophecy has surely been fulfilled, but their wisdom is lacking in Spirit consciousness, and general morality.

In order to regain at least a reasonable degree of control of our children, we must revitalize the age of discipline. It is extremely important to fill our children's minds to the limit of their intellectual ability. But we must also provide them with spiritual knowledge and wisdom, and give them something concrete to occupy, and fill the moral vacuum that the difficulty of modern existence has created. The empty space should be filled with an intimate relationship with God.

Those of us, who spends large sums of money, and time struggling to understand human behavior, will entertain many ideas that we consider to be rational solutions, but an established relationship with God is the only proven solution.

Have our social structure evolved to the point that we are so intelligent, so technologically advanced that we are unable, or unwilling to acknowledge the simple truth? You do not have to be a rocket scientist, or a prophet, to understand that if we fail to encourage our young people to seek and intimate relationship with God, our society's moral conscious and survival will surrender to atheism, barbarity, and ultimately non-existence.

Residual Benefits of
Black Slavery in America

BLACK SLAVERY IN AMERICA WAS one of the most wicked and cruel ordeals that any human being, group or race should be subjected to. To suggest that it could have had any degree of residual benefit to the total development of humanity may seem inconceivable, and insane.

Slavery is a fruit produced by the coupling of two natural flaws of human character. They are the desires to have power and supremacy. Whether we admit it or not, the difference between the slave and the slave owner is a matter of dominance.

Because I am a proud black male, a distant off spring of slaves, there is a natural reluctance to suggest that slavery was a matter of dominance. Admitting that my race was not technologically advanced enough to overcome the social forces that enslaved us is very humbling. Yet, reluctantly, I must admit that no individual or a society can enslave anyone, without the power to dominate. It was truly a matter of the survival of the fittest.

The Primal flaws interwoven into the fabric of human nature are not tools of evil, but when the desire for power and supremacy is the motivating factor, evil is encouraged to fester and grow.

All human lives are governed, or influence in some way by these natural cravings. If anyone, group, or nation has the power to exert their will upon others without major consequences, they will. It does not matter whether it is the smallest, primitive tribe, and individual, or a great nation.

Because I am an offspring of slaves, I dared asked myself a question. I asked if there were any benefits to humanity derived from the enslavement of black people in America. I concluded that the benefits were substantial and important.

Because the black race survived our ordeal, we encouraged a great nation in terms of its constitutional laws, the principles from which the formation of democracy stand on, and its role in the world's community of nations to examine its self. When we demanded that it examine its moral foundation, we coerced it into becoming a champion for universal civil liberties for humanity.

With our broken bodies, missing vital parts, and rope burns about our necks, we designed the template used to dislodge the chains of bondage from the existence of humankind. We accomplished this despite the blatant inhumanities that we were forced to endure.

Our political and social influence gradually evolved and created an atmosphere of intolerance to the bondage in South Africa, and many other oppressed non-white countries in the world. It allowed Bishop Tutu and others to illuminate the belly of the beast called apartheid. If the American black Race had not suffered and endured, no predominate, white society would have paid any attention to a race of black people in a foreign country, who were totally dehumanized by whites.

It is only rational for me to imply that the residual benefits derived from the bondage of the American black race altered the social, political, and behavioral response of human evolutionary progression. It is my conclusion that the fragile foundation of the universal social structure of humanity would not only be lopsided, but also morally bankrupt, as it relates to dark, skin human beings without the suffering, and the contributions of black America.

Angels of Mercy

While I lay in a hospital, as sore as a boil,

All around me, there was an uproar and turmoil.

I wondered what they had to gripe about.

Why there were people in the basement whose lights had been turned out.

Suddenly, I realized that they only cared about themselves.

They should have been patients in the nut ward upstairs.

Sometimes, I got tired of listening, but there was little else to do.

Oh how I wished they would talk about something new!

He said, she said, and things that did not matter,

Suddenly, there come the supervisor, oh, how quickly they scattered.

All along the ward, there were patients crying in vain.

I often heard them beg, "Nurse please ease the pain!"

It was clear that the angels of mercy just did not care.

However, one day their fate may change, and they will be lying here.

Crisis in America

THE CITIZENS OF AMERICA ARE faced with an enormous responsibility. We must retain, refine, and protect our moral heritage, our civil liberties and democratic principles. We have arrived at the crossroads of our nation's future. Social progression, our great technological advancements and our ability to sustain ourselves have contaminated our faith and weaken our need for a God that we cannot see or touch.

Our society has a multitude of God-fearing people, and yet, we are gradually abandoning a necessary component that purposes a rational guide to a humane existence. That component is morality. Morality is defined as conduct judged from a moral standpoint. It is the ability to recognize the difference between right and wrong, morality and immorality, and the desire to choose the former over the latter.

There are numerous social structures with various religious doctrines and beliefs that do not recognized the principles of the Holy Bible as a template for their moral conscience. Therefore, it is conceivable that the ideology of a particular social environment, the philosophical variations, and the social development of those environments determine the application of morality for that particular social environment.

The American system of governing is the fruit harvested from the moral and ethical principles found in the Holy Bible. It is indisputably obvious that God has given our nation the awesome responsibility as guardians of the world's communities. It is also apparent that he maintains and preserves our nation's existence and strength for the purposes of assuring the advancement of his moral principles and a refuge for the world's weary souls, and socially afflicted, despite our nation's continuing moral decay. It appears obvious that our nation's great power is supported by God as a guardian for the advancement of individual free will on our planet. However, if America ceases to embrace its moral responsibilities, atheism and barbarity will quickly consume the advancement of that free will, morality, and any other form of Godliness.

It is evident, that without the divine rules and principles that govern our democratic social structure, our moral obligation would not exist. Our freedom to worship and acknowledge the existence of a living God, his Son Jesus Christ, or any God that we choose, is what separates us from the rest of humanity's social ideologies. If our nation is to continue as the guardian of freedom, our citizens, and especially our children must embrace and shoulder this responsibility.

Our courts have decided to allow a few to dictate the places we can teach and exhibit our faith. These courts, under the influence of those few, have attempted to remove Godliness from every part of our society. The belief in a divine creation and the existence of God should be taught in the schools, the streets, and anywhere that a single individual will listen. The mere acknowledgment that God, his Son, our Lord and Savior Jesus Christ exists is the foundation that allows the possibility of compassion, and sound, moral, and ethical behavior.

There are multitudes of people who do not believe in the existence of a supreme being—Father or Son. They are defined as atheists, agnostics, and infidels. The mere fact that an individual does not acknowledge the existence of God deprives them of the moral sensitivity to govern their behavior response to any form of stimulus.

An atheist, a scientist, or anyone who do not believe that their total existence is part of a divine plan, has severed their moral connection to the remainder of humanity. Only the absolute fear of the wrath of God can impede the aggressive nature of human behavior.

Hills of Tennessee

In the hills of Tennessee, where I was born,

People can walk for miles and walk alone.

When you stand on top of Old Smokey,

With the cool breeze blowing gently along,

You get down on your knees before God,

And give thanks that this was your home.

Since I left home, I have traveled from place to place.

Whenever I am lonely, the mountain is always there.

I can feel its gentle breeze blowing through my hair.

There is no place I would rather be,

Than back home in the hills of Tennessee.

Politics Without Ethics
(The decline of an institution)

AMERICA IS TRULY A GREAT nation, anchored by an institution called democracy. The principles of this institution are a testament to its greatness. It has had the largest influence on the social evolution of humankind since the Roman Empire. But any social structure great or small is only as powerful as the vision and strong points of its leaders. Much like the leaders of those ancient empires, the factors that govern the survival or decline of any social structure depend on the ability of its leaders to shelve an abundance of crap up its citizen's unsuspecting rear ends.

Proud men die bravely for causes that a great majority of time, are not worth the blood trickling from a wound that a Band-Aid could cover. It is a natural form of genocide. We may not recognize the functioning of this flaw in our social structure, because it is hidden among the principles of protecting and defending our way of life. Wars and conflicts have been fought every since the world began, most often fueled by the petty desires of some leaders ego.

America's politicians are a shrew and greedy bunch. They often misuse the privileges that their political positions allow them, to create a base for power, corruption, and unscrupulous activities. When we choose an individual to be our representative in government, the individual is suppose to be our voice in the governing body. Instead, they use their positions to advance their own interest, and ill-gotten gains. Much too often, we are misrepresented. If we allow them to remain in office too long, we give them the opportunity to construct a base for power, consequently, reducing their concerned for the wishes of their constituents.

The great leaders of the past forged a struggling group of colonies, and social ideas into a functioning social structure. They were not infallible, but men of enormous character and convictions, regardless of their intrinsic values. Unfortunately, they failed to leave their secrets with us. I realize that today's problems are different and more complex, but the commitment to solving them should remain constant.

America's struggle for the survival of a free human existence depends greatly upon the wisdom and the foresight of our leaders, but each day, we discover that these individuals are very fragile ethically and morally, as the two words relate to social and political behavior.

The fundamental functioning of our nation often suffers from the lack of competent leadership. I wonder if among all of the modern politicians, an inkling of common sense could be salvaged. I suspect that if we removed the political rhetoric, and disguises, we would probably reveal that many of them are only greedy, self-centered, egotistical meatheads.

Our society not only tolerates their greed and selfishness, but also cultivates their deceptions, and incompetence for the sake of scandal. They are the embodiment of a society snared by the tentacles of greed, power, and social dominion, and they demonstrate a continual diminishing disregard for social and constitutional morality.

Our leaders must admit to their political bull, because they are no longer fooling anyone. Our citizens must observe this change to energize the pride, and the patriotism that has slowly diminished in our hearts. But before pride and patriotism can be restored, these people must renew their efforts to be competent.

The lust for power is a social malignancy that encourages unethical behavior. It represents one of the most serious threats to our nation's demise. Nuclear weapons cannot protect us from ourselves. Our nation's citizens seem to be stumbling through life with a dangerous insensitivity to what is actually taking place around us.

It is not the communist, the terrorist, or any other bunch of deranged degenerates that truly threaten our nation, but a rapidly collapsing political arena, where an idea, good or bad usually ignites a dogfight within our governing body.

I realize that the two party system keeps our social structure with some resemblance of balance, and a politician must be loyal most of the time to their own party's position. However, when their positions become petty and personal, the nation's business, and the well being of its citizens are much too often placed in needless jeopardy.

If our nation is going to continue as the guardian of democracy, its citizens must be able to rejuvenate our respect and trust in our political system. We cannot fight terrorism, or any other threat, if we do not trust the leadership that is in political power. It is difficult to regain respect and trust, when the individuals that we choose are discovered to be nothing more than common criminals. And while they are in office, we must not allow them to use their political position as a vehicle to establish a base for power.

If the system that allows the longevity of political representation is not changed, our future will be nothing more than a glimmer of light at the end of a long, dark tunnel. It will be bleak and unrecognizable.

In our dependence upon our leaders, we are behaving like fat sheep condemned to slaughter. We are accepting our fate, while waiting to be plunged into damnation.

We, as citizens must pay attention to what is actually happening in the world and in our nation. We have got to learn to discern between the lies, the deceptions, and the worthless, tactful device called diplomacy. The diplomacy that we are using is grossly outdated and dysfunctional and functions only as a tool to soothe the salvage breast. We cannot just stand by while the chosen few that we refer to as leaders guide our nation into financial, moral, and even spiritual bankruptcy in their abuse of this out dated political tool.

There is an enormous cloak of lies, deceptions, and worthless diplomacy that are the primary mechanisms that support the imminent demise of the freedoms that we once took for granted. The sum total of all our country's problems can be credited to these devices And now that the cancer called terrorism has attached its tentacles to the conscience of so-called civilized humanity, it feeds on our fears and uncertainties, and therefore enhances the necessity for more lies, deceptions and worthless diplomacy.

Humans are simply too flawed to obtain the wisdom to derail the motivation that fuels that malignancy. Like the onslaught of an acquire social disease, it will erode and impede the social progression of not only democratic principles, but any opportunity for a peaceful coexistence and the social advancement of humanity.

There are no quick fixes, and no brainstorming antidotes. It is clearly obvious that our nation and the peace loving world have its backs against the wall and the pressure will continue until we are push to the limit of our endurance.

All of our knowledge, creativity, resourcefulness, and thought to be unlimited power cannot stand against the forces of a social and religious indifference world. Free will cannot stand against a world where death, disease, and hunger does not take an occasion, but is the occasion. There are just too many people who do not value life, liberty, and the pursuit of happiness, simply because they have not experienced it.

Who are we to suggest and force any nation to accept democracy as a way of living? What gives us the right to bomb, kill and maim their families and demolish their homes and lives? Those of us who were alive will remember, and those still to be born will be taught, and understand what people whose lives are shattered by exhibitions of military power, called shock and awe feel. America cannot solve all the problems in the world, and yet, we cannot tolerate isolationism.

There is no quantity of Nuclear Weapons that can alter the erosion that will surely strain the very fabric of our social structure. And if we are consumed with the illusion that the political changing of the guard will make any perceivable variation in the near future, we are in for a rude awakening. The course has been set, and the clock is ticking.

The causation of past mistakes, and a world filled with deadly random probabilities that threaten not only the fundamentals of democracy, but the continual existence of humanity will surely prevail. Soon, we will be only able to recognize America by the remnants of its democratic principles.

The political mistakes are obvious, and there is plenty of blame that can be accredited to all involved. But what good would focusing on blame contribute to the solution. The questions are, have we as citizens learn anything? Do we understand that political power has limits? Do we understand the importance of checks and balances in our political system for either party, and that it was created to prevent even in a democratic social structure, a form of dictator ship fueled by political power? Do we understand that the people that we allow to govern us are human and subject to all the flaws and frailties like everyone else? Are we willing and strong enough to hold them accountable?

If we continue to embrace our social biases as a format for political preference, even the remnants of freedom will be severely diminished, or unavailable.

Recognition of Equality

Out of the shadows of slavery, a flame of intolerance still flickers.

Reluctantly, the black race is still stumbling through the dark caverns of social bondage; searching for acceptance, but we are held back by the elusive recognition of total equality.

Feminine Endurance

It is true that the female is equal.

All of God's children are.

Yet, there are some things that men can do that women will never measure up too.

Their brains are just as great as a man's, but their bodies are so delightfully soft and round.

I am sure that God did not intend for them to be bounced against the ground.

Heroes

What makes some people heroes?

Some would say that they are just fools.

Others would say that they are stupid people, who obviously lost their cool.

For an individual to be a hero, they must forget about themselves,

And for a moment in their life, they conquer the fear of death.

Marriage and the Modern Couple

THE DEFINITION OF MARRIAGE STATES that it is a social institution in which a male and a female are legally united to form a new family unit. It does not mention the word holy.

Marriage was once considered a holy bond. Although it is not stated in any dictionary, the holy bond was once regarded as an essential element of marital relationships, and was the primary link of the chain that binds the two individuals together. Although poetic expression has almost replaced holy, it is still used occasionally, but is slowly on its way out.

The success of every marriage depends upon the moral, composition of the links of its chain. The chains are forged from the essence of the marriage. The things that the individuals can and cannot do, the mutual respect, the golden rule, the willingness for unlimited, unconditional sacrifice, and the recognition of individual limitations, are all properties of the chain.

Out of the difficulty of modern existing, the moral aspects of marriage have succumbed to the complexity of social progression; including same sex marriages, thereby, threatening God's original plan, and even the institution of established marital relationships.

In the past, life was simpler. The male and the female were clearly identifiable according to their traditional roles. Both partners had more respect for the role that each other performed in the family unit.

The male ego has always relished the idea that the female was at least physically inferior. He was proud of his physical attributes that allowed him to accomplish certain tasks that a female could not, or was too feminine to attempt. When the female demanded equality in all phases of social evolution, she severely altered the male's way of thinking regarding their femininity. An enormous burden was placed upon him that challenged his manhood and purpose. Instead of loving, protecting, and taking care of the female, he became her social and economic rival.

Because the female no longer required the physical characteristics the male traditionally provided, he responded by being less devoted to her. Therefore, much too often, the only bond that binds the two genders together is intercourse. Unfortunately, intercourse is not a cohesive bond.

Both genders also object to the traditional vows of marriage. The modern concept is that the idea of an individual being compelled to live with another, in sickness and in health, until death, is an absolute, ridiculous commitment.

The Threshold of Equality

Black people are standing at the threshold of equality; yet, we fail to enter.

The dark covering that covers us conceals no blackness in our hearts.

We are equal, at least in the eyes of God.

Black and proud, we must stand together with our heads held high toward the clouds.

As we struggle to be socially equal, the threshold will open for you and me.

Damnation

HUMANITY HAS MADE GREAT SOCIAL strides in our brief attempt to achieve a reasonable level of civilization. Yet, despite the social advancements, we have allowed the deterioration of two of the most important elements of our social evolution. They are the value placed on human life and the degree of technological assistance that will be allowed to influence the quality of human existence.

It is evident that we are progressing technologically more quickly than we are capable of truly understanding the magnitude, and the direction of our progression. These tools are the products of social evolution. Unfortunately, they will surely determine the value of future human existence.

One of the greatest challenges to our survival is the technology we call the Internet. It is our master, and we are its slaves. Despite its ability to unite the world into a global community, there are imminent dangers and evil lurking in its shadows. Because the nature of men is continuously evil, there are enormous possibilities of these dangers, but we are reluctant to summit our resources to discourage the probability of a catastrophic happening.

Computers have taken total control of human existence with such ease that we are reluctant to examine any possibilities that will impede their progress. However, the people who have the power to monitor the possibilities of imminent danger should attach enormous significance to those dangers.

Human cloning is another social malignancy camouflaged by the pretense that it will somehow improve the natural function of human reproduction. The possibilities of disruption to the natural order of human reproduction are enormous and unimaginable.

The family unit is all ready in imminent danger of becoming obsolete in most modern social structures. If the progression of human cloning is allowed to continue, sex for the purpose of reproducing will be not only threatened, but severely crippled. It also has the potential to introduce another class of people into a world all ready bitterly divided by class.

I realize that it is ridiculously insane to suggest that any modern social structure of so-called rational human beings will allow such an incredible malignancy to grow. Yet, the decline of morals and ethics in all so-called civilized social structures are obvious. Cloning is a technology better left to other species of living things. And though, we are probably technologically capable of reproducing human beings by cloning, we are incapable of governing the integrity, direction, and the magnitude of that technology.

The vehicle that supports human development and social progression is primarily the family unit. If the normal relationship between the male and the female is interrupted any further than it already is, the fundamental ingredient of human reproduction and natural development, will eventually be polluted beyond it usefulness.

The right to die may be one of the most highly contested arguments in our immediate future. Death is a natural and personal encounter. It is the climax to the intimacy of existing. We are in awe, and yet most of us fear it.

There are a few social structures that place great value on human life. There are a growing number of people in primarily our so-called civilized, somewhat humane social structures who seek death as a means to overcome pain, suffering and loneliness. Still, there is an overwhelming number of people who value every breath. So we must be cautious and not allow this value to be lessened because the biological life support systems of individuals are no longer functioning normally. If we are not cautious, we encourage the possibility of the social regression of that value. The right to die may be an individual's fundamental right, but if it is allowed to attach itself to the conscience of a progressive social structure, it could spawn far-reaching consequences. Instead of allowing sick people to die, we will become less tolerant, or possibly merciless in an effort to save money and rid ourselves of the non-productive citizens that want to live. We have made great progress in understanding how to prolong life, but we are spiritually and socially unprepared to govern human longevity.

Genesis
"The dawn of madness"

In the beginning, the planet took shape and form; all was right in the eyes of God. The beast roamed the earth; the fowl soared, and the fish explored the infinite bowels of the watery depths. The planet was without sin and evil, conscience and morality. Humanity had not yet arrived.

Bone, flesh, and sinew were fashioned from the beast trodden earth's crust. Mighty hands cradled the dawning of man, then reached into his flesh, and ripped from his ribs, the beginning of madness.

Lost Innocence

A boy struggles to grow up in the projects without his dad.

His mom is a crack head.

His life is so sad.

He runs around with the neighborhood gang.

He learns to steal.

He was given a gun and taught to kill.

To survive, he sells dope.

He is trying to get on top.

He has great hope.

The welfare his mom gets goes up in smoke.

She turned him in, because he wouldn't credit her dope.

Each day is a struggle-he refuses to cry.

There is no one to care if the young man lives or dies.

Does God Exist?

THE BELIEF IN A SUPREME being is universal. However, there are as many different versions of religious doctrines as there are cultures. Nearly ever human acknowledges a presence in the universe that is greater than we are. But because of the social, environmental, and culture variation of humanity, and even superstition, the belief in this omniscient presence has many names, and functions in our lives. Therefore, an obvious question arises, when examining the spiritual dilemma of faith. The question is does it matter whether we refer to God as Jehovah, Allah, God, or any other name, as long as the individual acknowledges him as the only God? The greatest differences that determine the beliefs in a Supreme Being are scriptural interpretations, social environments, superstition, and culture variations. If God is the father of all things, does the difference in our reference to him diminish the truth of our faith?

It is not my intention to suggest that the beliefs of any group, culture, or faith are not valid, or that they are subordinate to my own. However, according to my Bible, the major difference is having faith in God's only begotten Son Jesus Christ, who is our living Savior and our only means to salvation. He also offers more of a rational guide to a humane existence.

The Holy Bible teaches us that God created the heavens and the earth, and reminds us that we must have faith in him, his Son, and the Holy Spirit, in order to believe that this event occurred. It also teaches us that his son Jesus came to earth to rescue humanity. If we have faith, through the shedding of his blood, our salvation and justification is assured. Common sense suggests that if an individual has to be reborn in the spirit, and totally deny his natural instincts for the sake of salvation, that faith in Jesus Christ is the true relationship we must search for.

There are quite a few culture-based religions that do believe in God as a Supreme Being, but faith in Jesus Christ is the ultimate difference. Why are we asked to have faith? Maybe it was because our intellect, arrogance, natural flaws and moral weaknesses would not allow us to worship a God that we could not see or touch. But if we cannot recognize God's presence functioning in our lives everyday, then neither faith nor anything else will convince us.

Many of us are eager to disprove the existence of a Supreme Being. Because we assume that we are the true guardians of our destinies, we believe that there can be nothing in the universe greater than we are.

Is it not ridiculous to gaze upon the complexity of creation, and not be able to perceive a divine presence? If we allowed ourselves to use the simple principle of being rational, we would clearly understand that the universe is a divine conception, rather than just an accident. We can observe God's presence in every mystery of creation that is within the realm of our perception, if we looked just beyond our daily environmental existence.

Because of an expanding gap between science and religious philosophy, humanity, particularly Christians will be infinitely deprived of understanding the phenomenon that occurs in God's universe. This phenomenon was set in place by a living God. Even beyond faith, there simply is no other valid explanation.

The modern scientific community suggests that the application of differential equations, calculus and some of their relatives are the only means to investigate these mysteries. They suggest that these equations are the primary vehicles in which the truth is obtainable.

Now I will admit that there are physical laws that govern every function that occur in our universe. Since the foundation for mathematics is logic, some of these functions can be elevated to the realm of rational perception by applying differential equations, or many of the other mind-boggling mathematical systems. However, these equations will never be the vehicles to reveal the absolute truth, even for some of the mysteries that are not as complex as creation.

We can gaze into the infinite vastness of space forever. We can continue to unearth the ancient bones and relics, but we will never get any closer to unveiling the truth of creation using the vehicles that we have devised. Truth is perfection and need not be altered, or changed. But from the beginning of man's inquiry of metaphysics, to the modern physics applications, the presentation of accepted scientific speculation has been periodically upgraded.

The scientific approach to truth in regard to the physical functioning of the universe in its infancy was primarily supported by the non-Euclid axioms of geometry. These axioms were the basic for the evolution of all modern physics inquiries. It is true that its descendants, geometry, differential equations, and other forms of mathematics are valid tools that are capable of explaining to some degree many of the mysteries of the universe, but a great number of their interpretations are not self-evident, or intelligible, or even logical. Much too often, they do not make sense, even to those who try to cram their conclusion down our unsuspecting throats.

Operational definitions, differential equations, and other mathematics are tools created by man. And although they are primarily based on logic, they are much too volatile and variable to obtain the absolute truth. Therefore, I must conclude that any form of mathematics is not flawless, and does not possess infinite validation.

The foundation for scientific argument is that geometry and its descendants are vehicles to obtain intelligible facts. If they are not flawless, they cannot produce an explanation of anything in a manner that can be viewed as the absolute truth, especially a mystery that is so complex that the Bible reminded us to employ faith.

To a reasonable intelligent human being the suggestion that the universe simply exploded, and that every mystery that supports the planet and life on it happened by chance is ridiculously irrational. If we observe the functioning of our planet, the properties that governs it, and life in it, we would discover that it functions on cause and effect, probability, and random variables. But God who is the greatest mathematician created the heavens and the earth, and controls everything that he created.

Probability is a principle of logic. Every event that occurs in the cosmos/heavens and on earth has a probable value that is attachable to it. The weather forecasters, earthquake scientists, and many of the other natural event forecasters use the principles of random probability. Every event that occurs in the universe has a probable value that can be determined by the sum of its possibilities, and the collective or set that limits the occurrence to a finite value.

A doctor tells his heart patients that if they do not loose weight, and stop eating foods with high cholesterol contents, there is a certain probability that they will have seriously health problems, or even die. In sociology, a parent tells their misbehaving child that if they do not stop hanging out with bad crowds, they are probably going to be in trouble with the law or dead. These are just general statements about the relationship of probable cause and effect in all branches of science, and other related functions.

To understand an event that occur in our universe, on earth, and in our environment, I will assign certain events as random variables. Variables are things that are apt to be changed. The birth and the death of planets; the expanding universe; life, death, social progression and regression are all products of probability and random variables. Even the evolutionary social progression of the human race is a product of these principles. The development of families is a random variable. This variable and probability determine our choice of mates and every function of the family relationship thereafter.

There will never be a super computer, an individual or group, smart, wise, or knowledgeable enough to associate the enormous number of variables to the forces that truly govern our existence, our planet or the universe. Only God knows the answers.

Some scientist suggests that the universe expanded from the explosion of a single molecule—the big bang theory. That is truly stretching the theory of creation beyond the boundaries of rational speculation. However, as far as the big bang theory is concerned, anything is possible with God; therefore, it also carries a probable value. I do not possess the knowledge, nor does anyone else to prove, or disprove that a big bang occurred. As for me, I trust in the word of God.

There are unlimited opinions to the dilemma of creation, but common sense, faith, and the simple function of attempting to be rational allow us only two. Is the creation of the universe and the formation of life an accident, or divine involvement? Regardless of how these events occurred, there was a divine purpose for their creation.

Time is a major factor of disagreement between science and religion. But regardless of the infinite amount of time allotted to creation and human progression, truth will depend upon on our faith, the moral values that we attach to human existence, and the principles from which we obtain those values.

We will not be able to unravel events that took place at the beginning of creation, by applying formulas, differential equations, operational definitions, laws, principles, or the visiting of alien beings. Any conclusions that anyone or I may reach will be purely theoretical, and supported only by our faith, or any other vehicle that we used to arrive at our conclusions.

It is not difficult to understand that every function in the universe and on the planet is interrelated. Realizing this, even without faith, enables the probability of a creator. The seemly unlimited ability of modern science has failed to produce any other rational explanation.

It is obvious that someone greater than any human being influenced the spirit of man to write the Holy Scriptures found in the Bible. This should be clear to any individual with a tidbit of common sense.

While it is a true statement that man wrote the Bible, only a tiny bit of simple reasoning would reveal that we did not conceive its principles. No human being has ever possessed the wisdom, the foresight, love and kindness, and the concern for the well being of humanity printed on its pages.

The Bible teaches that God created the heavens and the earth. To a scientist, this statement would provoke a response of tautological or dogmatic. But they cannot prove that he did not.

It makes no difference who we are, where we live, or the forces that govern our existence, if we have the opportunity to be exposed to the words in the holy Bible, we will recognize that they are the only truth.

Maybe we think that we are too smart, or we may be too stupid, or even a combination of both, to allow ourselves to see the divine plan and engineering of a perfect universe.

The scientific community wants us to believe that the universe simply exploded, and that it had no purpose except that a single molecule or a bunch of solar gases ignited. They want us to believe that our planet accidentally inherited the environment, and the resources that were necessary to create and sustain an infinite number of different living organisms that are totally dependent on their environment.

Because our bodies are an assembly of complex organic cells that replicates, it was also speculated that humanity began as an assortment of replicating DNA cells, a primordial soup or so-called gene pool. Such a statement only contributes more confusion to the spirit of uncertainty in those who support their Godless beliefs, and has no other value. Since there are other complex organisms on our planet, it is ridiculously insane to suggest that these microscopic cells could randomly select the type of organisms that they would form. However, if this idea had any degree of truth, then there must have been a vast amount of confused DNA running around looking for something to create.

When the Bible said that God created the heavens and the earth, and everything in it, he did not mention how he did it, except to say that he spoke it into existence. For the sake of argument, I will acknowledge that it is possible that the big bang may have occurred. It is also possible that the universe as we understand it was a direct result of this event. Yet, there is no doubt that creation was not an accident, and someone greater than man had a plan. If we examined every function in the universe that are within the realm of our perception; the organic, and the inorganic elements that makes up our planet, we would discover the wondrous design of that plan.

The Bible said that each new generation of humans would be weaker and wiser than the previous ones. Historical documentation of human behavior will bare witness of a total decline in moral values in our so-called civilized social structures, while our intellect has unimaginably soared. It is written that the seasons would change so drastically it would be difficult to recognize one from the other. God said that the desires of man's hearts would be continually evil. This truth is as universally plain as the noses on our faces. God gave man dominion over all that he created. He said that we would live by the sweat of our brow, and that the role of the female would be to bare fruit. All of these predictions and more are from the pages of the Bible.

It does not matter how smart we are, our beliefs or doubts, if we allow a tiny bit of common sense to enter into our attempt to reason, we would discover that these predictions are valid.

We can argue about who wrote the Bible, and its origin. We can debate its truths, and its relevance to the evolutionary behavioral response of humanity. Still, we cannot deny that the words that are printed on its pages are not the closes mankind has ever come to the true.

Nostradamus was a French astrologer who predicted events that he believed would occur in the world long after he ceased to exist. He was nothing more than a human being that studied astrology. Still, his predictions are scrutinized with the assumptions of unchallenged validity.

God predicted events in the social, evolution of mankind that has occurred, and will continue to occur until the end of days. However, our supposedly greatest minds would rather lend themselves to the forecasting of a human being rather than God. I have never heard it mention that Nostradamus' predictions were subjected to the axioms of geometry, or any of its glorified relatives.

The application of logic is the science of pure reasoning. It is a way of arguing the predictability by which certain causes have certain effects. The fundamental functioning of nature is a convincing testimony to the application of the principles of logic. The pages of the Bible are filled with logical principles that are guidelines to live by. The supreme entity that created the heavens and the earth was a logical, Spiritual being. Since man was created in his spiritual image, we were also given the ability to be logical.

I could fill this book with words explaining how from the beginning of scientific inquiry to the modern technological advancements, how man has utilized the principles of logic. Yet, if we are so ridiculously intent on not using faith or even the simple act of reasoning to discover the truth, and we continue to invent reasons to disprove the existence of a divine creation, then only the inevitable reality of a collision with God will convince us of his existence.

Necessary Evil

THE EXISTENCE FOR THE BLACK race in America to say the least has been an infinite struggle. To imply that we are due social reparations is subordinate to the compensations that are truly owed us.

Affirmative action is a social tool created as an attempt to repair and compensate the damage done by past discrimination. Although it is necessary, it is an enormous obstacle to racial tolerance.

Any form of discrimination, whether it be reversed, or fueled by bigotry is morally and socially counter productive. It impedes the progression of social tolerance and coexistence. Still we must proceed with this practice for as long as its function is valid, and our society tolerates it.

Unfortunately, the social barriers that created the need for reverse discrimination are still in place. I can understand the rage, and frustration that a young white individual must feel when they are told that they are going to be left out because of the color of their skin. Black people are intimately familiar with this practice. The discrimination conditions the young whites for the coercing of hate groups that use their frustration to recruit them.

Black people must not become dependent on affirmative action to substitute for hard work. In order to be socially equal, and participate in our society, we must demonstrate that we can compete, and be equal to the task. As long as we allow white people, or any other people to claim that they are smarted than we are, the forces of social gravity will continue to staple our feet to the lowest rung of the social ladder.

We must not allow anyone, group or race to sabotage our abilities and intellect because we were place in a position because of the color of our skin. Although affirmative action is morally wrong and counter productive to social co-existence, it is still absolutely necessary to the advancement of blacks and other minorities in our society.

Black people are generally great athletes that have produced quite a few millionaires. Sadly, we have been influence into believing that the black race has overcome. We assume that if we excel in sports, we do not have to study. Simply because we can run faster and jump higher than most athletes of other races, we think that learning is not a requirement for social advancement. This assumption is not valid. If we are going to stop the hasty generalizations of our race, the indifference and the social dominance, we cannot rely upon any other vehicle accept education and focus to help us to overcome.

The Relationship
Between Love, Respect, and Trust

LOVE PERFORMS AN IMPORTANT ROLE in the social and behavioral relationship between human beings. Webster's definition of love implies that it is a strong, passionate emotional feeling. This definition is partially accurate; however, emotion and passionate feelings are not the primary factors that produce the ingredient necessary for people to love each other. The primary ingredient for any relationship is respect. It provides a concrete foundation for a lasting and peaceful coexistence.

There are many kinds of relationships, families, friends, lovers and nations, each of them requiring respect and trust. Both respect and trust is often sacrifice, intentionally, or unintentionally for the fruits of passion, but love cannot exist without them.

Passion is not love, nor can it replace love, but it is the effect of unbridled emotions. It is a supplemental element of human behavior, and is only an outpouring of animal desire that is usually camouflaged by fantasy. It is immune to the principles of rational scrutiny, and is not essential to the formation of love.

The relationship between two individuals who are attracted to each other does not begin with love, unless the element of respect and trust has all ready entered into the relationship.

Humans are more family oriented than most of the species in the animal kingdom. The love for a family member is a product of kinship. Genes serves as an insulator to buffer the need for respect. We usually heap a generous share of love on family members regardless of their frailties.

The foundation for friendship is respect. A buddy, a pal, or any other relationship does not guarantee respect. Because there are a number of variables that encourage a relationship between nations, respect is often difficult to obtain. Much too often force is the tool used to gain respect by most nations. If it is obtained by force, it is usually tainted by fear or rage, and is therefore not valid.

The simple act of not having respect for other people is the fundamental reason why human beings are incapable of loving each other for the sake of it. We do not have the will to overcome the natural flaws, and social conditioning that overlaps our fragile, precondition desires to coexist.

Crime, Punishment
and Behavioral Modification

To CONTINUE TO EVOLVE AS a civilized species, humanity must attempt to maintain order in our environments. The numerous variations of social structures require that each employ their interpretations of behavior modifications to achieve this goal.

Some social structures do not recognize the basic rights of human beings. They have an assortment of cruel, inhuman penalties for committing a crime. While it is true that these penalties are powerful deterrents, they overlap humane considerations, and breach the realm of barbarity. Chopping an individual's hand off for stealing, or removing a testicle for rape is a deterrent that will surely influence a behavioral modification. But it is clearly an act that exceeds the boundaries of civilized justification.

In the more socially and technologically advance societies we at least make an effort to approach crime and punishment in a humane way. For the most part, we assume that an individual is innocent until proven guilty, and we allow the due processes of law to determine guilt or innocence, and the punishment to fit the crime.

For the most severe, socially intolerable crimes, we have capital punishment. The history of the relationship between crime and punishment reveals that it is not a deterrent, nor does it appear to be morally justifiable. However, in a social structure assembled primarily from morals based on Judean Christian principles and a democratic form of governing, the degree of the punishment must correspond to the gravity of the crime.

An eye for an eye may seem cruel and unusual punishment to people not directly affected by a crime. Yet, to a family of a victim, whose eye was plucked out, cruel and unusual punishment allows the possibility for justice and closure.

Democracy is a system that lends itself to the woes of social crimes. Our justice systems and prisons are overloaded. Because we seem unwilling to admit that our natural instincts influence our behavior, we will never understand the chronological association between human behavior, and crime.

Our technical skills and any other skills that we have that separate us from the remainder of the animal kingdom do not alter this fact. We are instinctually compelled to behave like animals from birth, and our total existence is governed by this biological truth.

Humanity

EARTH IS THE HOME OF an enormous diverse variation of species of animals. A natural bond, a mutual dependence for the continuation of the other, binds every species. The same primal laws govern us all. There are no distinct variations in the behavioral display of any species, as it relates to the primal laws of the survival of the fittest, and natural selection.

We marvel at the massive bodies of the dinosaurs. We also create mind-numbing images of their existence on earth with their vicious, predatory instincts. However, the human animal is the most dangerous, destructive, predatory species that ever walk upon the earth. There has never been an animal as vicious, cunning and dangerous as man.

Yes, we are superior in many ways, and yet we are inferior in others. The human brain is the only biological instrument that determines the gap between man and the other species. It also provides the flaws that lessen our biological advantage.

These natural flaws are tools that impede our ability to be rational. With all of the tools for survival that we possess, we are a species on the verge of eradication. We do not have the wisdom, or the desire to respond to the urgency that imminently threatens our existence.

Human beings are supposed to have the ability to be rational. If that is so, then we must find the courage to attempt to change our catastrophe, human dilemma.

The human puzzle offers two basic principles that are significant to any possibility for change. First, we must agree on who we are. If we manage to agree on the first principle, then we must attempt to discover why we are, or for what purpose are we. The uncovering of these seemly unobtainable elements may allow us to have a better understanding of human behavior, but the probability of agreement is very remote.

We are simply animals in nature, no more and no less. That is the only rational answer. If we agree that we are simply animals, then we can compare our behavior to the behavior of any other predatory species in the animal kingdom.

Why we are, or what is our reason for existing, is related to the fundamental functioning of all living things. Except for obedience to God, who created us in his Spiritual image, our primary function, as it is to all animals, is simply to reproduce and provide the continuation of our species. Everything else we do, discover, or create, are nothing more than the product of our intellect, and the unique structure of our biological life support system.

To admit that we are simply animals do not diminish our claim to being human; for it is only our behavior that lessens our humanity.

Human behavior is a functioning of the entity that we call the soul. Its primal flaws, the variation of social structures, the degree of morality, and environmental coercing are the elements that determine our behavior response.

A newborn human infant is merely a cute, cuddly little animal with only the capacity for a soul. Aside from our basic human instincts, we are born with undeveloped souls. The development of an individual's soul relies upon the individual's health, parental guidance, religious convictions, social and environmental conditioning.

The Erosion of Civilization

HUMANITY'S CONTINUOUS SKIRMISHES WITH EXTERMINATION have almost reached its climax. The combined minds of the world's greatest leaders, think tanks, and philosophers are unable to understand the natural principles that govern human existence.

When human beings are born, we are chronologically programmed to sustain the imminent danger that now threatens us. We are doomed because our very nature diminishes our ability to consider the well being of our fellow human beings. We are consumed by the craving for power, and dominion. Reluctantly, I must declare that there is not very much that we can do about the way things are.

If there is any degree of optimism to be salvaged, it is easily overwhelmed by an even greater degree of understanding that humanity truly does not have the ability to lend ourselves to the simple principles that could save us. Our natural instincts and the flaws that govern our behavior simply will not permit us to overcome the probability of the chaotic disruption to the advancement of civilization.

For as long as the world has stood, people have been killing each other, often without any degree of rational justification. This natural flaw in human beings appears immune to reasoning, or morality. The Primal forces that impede our desires to peacefully, coexist compel us to maim and murder each other, regardless of the degree of our civilization, or our declaration of morality.

We use many vehicles to camouflage our predacious intent. Wars fought for non-existing reasons, and genocide or ethic cleansing is just a few. We are animals and our behavior is influence by our natural cravings.

Now that the world is overflowing with nuclear proliferation, every social structure, large or small declares that they have the means to ultimate self-preservation. To gain attention from the international community, they threaten to blow each other away. Common sense would suggest that these societies are not stupid. If they are foolish enough to nuke each other over a few acres of dirt, they are far less civilized than the amount of time the existence of their particular social structures suggests. No society in their right mind, regardless of what kind of dictator or any other leadership in charge wants to die. Nuclear war is a no win situation.

Religion is an exhausted tool used to camouflage our natural craving to kill each other. The sum of human suffering and death in the name of religion is enormous. The progression of human social evolution is a monument and testament to that continuing unfortunate occurrence.

The conflict in the Middle East is an example of such a struggle. It began like a snowball rolling down the side of a snow covered hill. It kept getting larger and larger until it became insurmountable. It grew because what may have began as a dispute over territory evolved into hate. Hate hardens the heart and is continuous; it sustains the conflict, because generation after generation of Muslims has been taught that Israel is the enemy and is an illegitimate occupier of their land. There has never been, and there never will be peace in that Holy Land until no Jew trod upon the sacred soil that fuels the struggle.

The tussle for the occupation of the land in the Middle East is a camouflage to deceive the world. As I mentioned, there will never be peace until the blood of the Jews flows like a crescent river through the Holy Land into the Mediterranean.

Hate, pure and simple, is the fundamental motive that fuels the conflict. If a snake is a snake, we must call it that and recognize its threat, rather than summit to silly diplomacy that threatens the continuation of our own social ideologies.

The greatest danger to the existence of all living things, is the degree of probability that war-mongering countries like Russia and China will choose sides, just to prove to world that they too are players in the global power struggle.

America's governing political party appears hell-bent on destruction. Ultimately, that factor is going to determine the foreseeable functioning of any form of humane existence. While they were licking their chops in expectation of an easy struggle in Iraq, they tried to convince its citizens, whose lives they had destroyed, and would continue to destroy that what they are doing was for their benefit.

If you are going to drop bombs on someone's head, it is arrogant, and grossly dimwitted to suggest that they reward you with jubilation. It is truly obvious that these political leaders did not weigh the catastrophe consequences of their decisions. They will not be content until the blood of the enemy, young Americans, and our allies paint the sand of the mighty desert.

It is much too easy to send other people's children to sacrifice their lives, when the true justification is weighted with corrupt, political, greedy, power mongering politicians. Because the checks and balances of our governing body has eroded, our nation has committed to a struggle where there is an enormous probability there is no end.

With relative ease, we may be able to destroy so-called enemy states, or small nations. But if we are not cautious the intangibility of terrorism will dissolve the ingredients of our free society, and its fundamental functioning.

Understanding Human Nature

ALL HUMANS ARE PRIMARILY THE same. We are chronologically bonded, possessing similar flaws and wickedness. The color of one's skin, their social structures, environments, or social positions does not alter that fact.

If we believe in God, we believe that humans are the descendants of Adam and Eve, and therefore subject to the consequences of their actions. But if we are Christians, we believe not only in the existence of God, but also that his Son Jesus is the difference in how we perceive the workings of God. If we are not Christians, we are spiritually unprepared to comprehend the truth that truly governs human existence.

I believe in a living God, his Son Jesus, and the Holy Spirit. But by no means am I suggesting that anyone or any culture should conform to my faith. Yet, the only vehicle for understanding and repairing human behavior is to examine the words of the creator of all things. If something is broken, or do not function properly, we usually consult the original manufacturer. When humans need repair, we consult doctors, but they are merely technicians, not the creator. God made provisions in his word to take care of our every need.

I understand the overwhelming desire to disprove the existence of God the creator, and in particular Jesus Christ. When God created humans with the ability to elevate our minds beyond the need for rational thinking, he permitted us to challenge not only the authenticity of his word, but his existence. It is sad that so many brilliant minds will not experience ultimate joy, because of their continual attempt to offer irrational and often bizarre conclusions. I had no idea that cerebral superiority complexes excluded the presence of common sense.

There is but one God. Still, for the purpose of the God given right of choice, I will not condemn, nor will I condone the false gods that contaminate a large sum of human existence. However, it is obvious that we are unable to behave as a species with any concern for the welfare of others without an intimate relationship with Christ, and the desire to commit to his teaching.

Money and power is a double-edged sword that fuels the chaotic behavior of human kind. The two edges of this sword govern the functions of human behavior with equal ability.

It is extremely difficult for an individual, or a society to surrender to principles that are against our very nature. It is not in our character to love each other for the sake of it. There is a naturally reluctance to obedience, and subservience to a God that we cannot see or touch, whose rewards can only be fully available after we die. Therefore, if we have not accepted the teachings of Jesus Christ, all of the principles I mentioned above, will be beyond our reach.

To rectify and bridle human behavior, we must surrender to the teaching of Jesus Christ. When we allow our natural instincts to influence our behavioral responses to any type of stimuli, our capacity to behave wisely is compromised.

Just Another Nigger

THERE ARE DIFFERENT RULES FOR blacks and whites in America's social structure. I realize that this fact is nothing new. But when we as blacks entertain the illusion that our race has overcome, we omit the difficulty of the existence that still governs and overwhelms the bulk of our race.

The city that I call home is undergoing a constant, natural development. It is moving on up, so to speak. I love this city, and I am truly proud of that fact. However, beside the mutual love for the local college and pro basketball teams, it is a city divided, not just simply by race, but by the variation in the social and humane respect given to each race.

The different standards of respect for blacks and whites is nothing new in this city, or any other city in America where there is a great racial divide. But it has always been my assumption, that even though we are socially separate, the rules that supposedly govern a particular social structure breach the boundaries of race, geographies, and economics.

The police in most of America's cities treat blacks as if the colors of our skin automatically confirm our guilt. They ride into the so-called hoods like the Gestapo police, and overuse their authority, often without reasonably justification. `

They behave as if the humanity of black people is somehow diminished because of the environment in which a large sum of us exists. It appears that race, economics, and geographies, are vehicles used to determine the value and quality of black citizens.

The mere fact that economics allows individuals or groups to construct their natural habitats in environments outside the city limits does not confirm, or enhance the quality and value of those individuals, or groups.

The principles that govern the quality and value of human beings are not formed by economics, race, or geographies. If the political governing bodies were dominated by established white bureaucracies, the conclusions that I have reached could be easily justified. But the sad, reality is that a sizeable sum of America's cities both large and small is controlled by blacks.

The Decline Of An Empire
(The Rule of the Trojan horse)

GREAT NATIONS ONCE SETTLED THEIR differences with mortal combat. Nations were against nation's and allies choosing sides—human struggle; man against man—blood, carnage, and sacrifice. These were the methods by which war was carry out, when men were men, not cowards lurking behind the cloak of citizenship, businessmen, doctors and other occupations, camouflaged for the purpose of inflicting maximal damage to the purity of innocence, and the progression of freewill. This is the rule of terrorism. These men and women are Trojan Horses. Their weapon is terror. Terror dissolves the inherited sensation of safety from enemy combatants in our homeland that democracy once provided.

For all intent and purpose, the war against terrorism on all fronts is lost. Our nation is under seizing. That should be clear to everyone. Our society is in bondage to the uncertainty of terrorism, and every single segment our democratic principles are under its influence. Our reliance on our government to protect has eroded, and fear and distrust are the principles that occupy our lives daily. 9/11 designed the template for that frame of thought.

Hidden behind the disguises and religious mumbo jumbo of the terrorist is the manifestation of the truest composition of evil. They receive their glory in the suffering of innocence. God forbid that what they stand for has anything to do with righteousness. What we must realize is their objective is to win by any means necessary. They cannot defeat our military directly. But their strategy is not to stand directly against a greater force, but to defeat the hearts, and minds with fear, and therefore the will of their enemies' citizens by indirect confrontation. The substance of our freedoms are being siphon off by the very nature of terror's uncertainty and intimidation.

War is war, but the acceleration of terror is an evil against civilization, and innocence, and it contaminates the delicate balance of the peaceful coexistence of humanity, and has nothing to do with religion. This malignance has attached its tentacles to the conscience of every human being who do not share their agenda.

But terrorism comes in many forms. Great nations blatantly misuse their power in the name of some ideological premise that their form of governing is the blueprint for all global social environments. They call this form of terrorism, the preservation of their global interest, and social ideologies, but its only purpose is to enhance the evolution and survival of their own particular environments.

Mother Nature

The adorning of a summer shroud, Mother Nature dressed in green.

God created the heaven and the earth, and then crowned her the mighty queen.

She enables the change in seasons and the mighty storms that roar.

Mother Nature is God's tool. Oh, how I do love her so.

Joy and Peace

While I huddled underneath the old China Berry tree,

Dead man's alley was just across the path.

I saw the waste of human life, Oh God, I felt so sad.

From dawn until dawn, up and down the path they trod,

Looking for the joy and peace, found only in the grace of God.

Great Performances

I watched the robins' mating dance,

And the black birds gobbling up all they can.

The jaybirds were during the tippy-toe.

A sparrow watching from the branch of a willow tree,

Cheered them on for more.

I heard a mocking bird singing;

A sharp, C flat, or something like that.

Great performances on a summer day,

Encore, encore, I never had to say,

For they will perform tomorrow the same old way.